United States
Department of
Agriculture

Forest Service

Forest
Products
Laboratory

Research
Paper
FPL–RP–675

Hygrothermal Analysis of Wood-Frame Wall Assemblies in a Mixed-Humid Climate

Samuel V. Glass

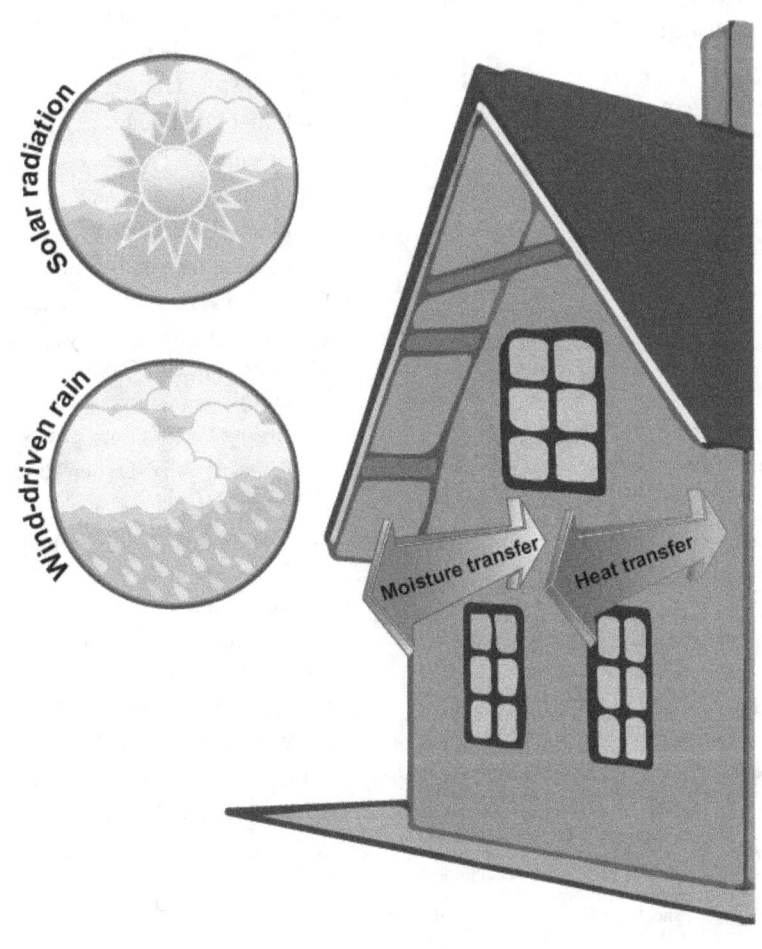

Abstract

This study uses a one-dimensional hygrothermal model to investigate the moisture performance of 10 residential wood-frame wall assemblies in a representative mixed-humid climate location of Baltimore, Maryland (climate zone 4A). All the assemblies include oriented strandboard (OSB) sheathing and vinyl siding. The walls differ in stud cavity thickness, level of cavity insulation, presence and type of exterior insulation, and class of interior vapor retarder. The performance of the wall assemblies is compared in four respects. First, seasonal trends in moisture, humidity, and temperature conditions are investigated, and the potential for wintertime moisture accumulation in OSB sheathing from vapor diffusion is assessed. Second, the rate at which OSB sheathing is able to dry from a high initial moisture content is compared for each wall assembly at four different times of year. Both the vapor diffusion and drying performance studies include sensitivity analyses to gauge the extent to which simulation results depend on various input parameters. Third, the response of OSB moisture content to wind-driven rain intrusion is examined. Finally, the contribution of air exfiltration to wintertime moisture accumulation in OSB sheathing is evaluated.

Keywords: Hygrothermal analysis, moisture performance, simulation, durability, building envelope, wood-frame, oriented strandboard, wind-driven rain, air leakage

April 2013

Glass, Samuel V. 2013. Hygrothermal analysis of wood-frame wall assemblies in a mixed-humid climate. Research Paper FPL-RP-675. Madison, WI: U.S. Department of Agriculture, Forest Service, Forest Products Laboratory. 25 p.

Acknowledgments

This study was supported by the NAHB Research Center through the U.S. Department of Energy Building America Program and by the USDA Forest Products Laboratory (FPL). This report was improved by critical comments from Joe Wiehagen and Vladimir Kochkin of the NAHB Research Center, C.R. Boardman of FPL, and Anton TenWolde, formerly of FPL.

Contents

Hygrothermal Analysis of Wood-Frame Wall Assemblies in a Mixed-Humid Climate

Samuel V. Glass, Research Physical Scientist
Forest Products Laboratory, Madison, Wisconsin

1. Introduction

Moisture performance is a key consideration in building envelope design. The occurrence of moisture problems resulting from poor design, construction, or unexpected interactions of new building materials can lead to a host of undesirable consequences: wood decay, mold growth, poor indoor air quality, infestation and degradation by insects, corrosion of metals, loss of thermal resistance in wet insulation, damage to materials and finishes from expansion or contraction, and loss of strength in building materials to the point of structural failure. Building repairs and litigation incur considerable costs.

Designers have many options in contemporary wood-frame wall construction when it comes to selecting materials such as exterior cladding, insulation, and vapor retarders. Building codes have recently required higher insulation levels, and in some cases continuous exterior rigid insulation may be an option or a requirement, depending on climate zone. Moisture performance is a multi-faceted issue; desirable performance includes avoiding moisture accumulation from bulk water intrusion, air leakage, and vapor diffusion, as well as having some degree of "forgiveness" such that assemblies have the ability to dry out if they get wet (either during construction or during their service life). The construction industry is currently not in agreement when it comes to the implications of exterior rigid foam insulation. For example, although exterior insulation can warm sensitive materials such as wood structural sheathing during cold weather and reduce the risk of condensation (Straube 2011), many practitioners question the risk involved in limiting the drying potential of the wall with vapor-impermeable foam (Gibson 2010). This issue involves many considerations, and moisture performance can depend strongly on the climate and the type of cladding, for example. This study attempts to clarify the various aspects of moisture performance by comparing 10 different residential wood-frame wall assemblies using hygrothermal modeling.

Hygrothermal analysis is a tool for evaluating the temperature and moisture conditions that might occur within a building envelope assembly over time. Such analysis can improve the understanding of how the building envelope responds to the interior and exterior environment and can identify potential moisture performance problems (such as those mentioned above). An important concept in hygrothermal analysis is that of "load." This term is used in hygrothermal analysis in the sense of a burden or demand on the building; the response of the building to the loads can be analyzed, and the performance can be judged to be acceptable or unacceptable (TenWolde 2011). Hygrothermal loads are analogous to loads in structural analysis (e.g., snow load, dead load, wind load) and to heating and cooling loads (sensible and latent loads) in mechanical system design. Hygrothermal loads include initial moisture levels in building materials; indoor temperature and humidity levels; outdoor conditions such as temperature, humidity, wind, rain, and solar radiation; and air pressure differences across the building envelope.

This section provides a brief background on moisture sources, moisture transfer mechanisms, moisture-related properties of wood, performance thresholds, and methods of hygrothermal analysis.

1.1 Moisture Sources and Moisture Transfer

Moisture can come from a variety of sources interior or exterior to the building; it can also come from wet materials in newly constructed buildings, such as fresh concrete, green lumber, and wet-applied insulations (Christian 2009). Indoor moisture sources include people, pets, plants, combustion, cooking, dishwashing, showering, bathing, cleaning, washing and drying of clothing, damp foundations, mechanical humidification, swimming pools, saunas, fountains, etc. Outdoor sources include rain, fog, dew, snow, humid air, and soil moisture. Leaks caused by the failure of building materials can occur inside or outside a building.

Moisture migration can occur through a number of pathways. For building physics applications, the most important are the following (Kumaran 2009; Karagiozis 2001):

- Liquid water can be transported in a number of ways: gravitational flow, liquid diffusion driven by a difference in moisture content, and capillary flow driven by suction pressure. An example of the latter is water absorption in porous claddings wetted by wind-driven rain, such as masonry, stucco, or wood.

- Water vapor can be transported by the flow of air (convection). This includes air leakage through unintended gaps in the building envelope, such as at electrical outlets and around windows, doors, light fixtures, and pipes. This also includes convective looping within wall cavities with low-density fibrous insulation.

- Water vapor can migrate by diffusion, driven by a difference in the partial pressure of water vapor (hereafter called "vapor pressure"). The material parameter associated with vapor diffusion is known as vapor permeability.

Wetting can occur through any of these mechanisms. Drying can occur by air flow and vapor diffusion. Liquid transport can also redistribute moisture from a wet region over a larger volume.

1.2 Moisture-Related Properties of Wood and Wood Products

All the wall assemblies analyzed in this study are of wood-frame construction and include oriented strandboard (OSB) sheathing. A brief overview of some important moisture relations is provided here; for further information, see Carll and Wiedenhoeft (2009) and Glass and Zelinka (2010).

Moisture content (MC) is defined here as the ratio of the mass of water in a given volume of dry material to the mass of the same volume of material in an oven-dry condition, expressed either as a decimal or as a percentage. A number of properties of wood depend on moisture content, such as dimensional shrinkage and swelling, strength, moisture transfer, and thermal properties. Water can exist in wood in the liquid or vapor phase in the cell lumina (cavities) or as bound water in the adsorbed phase within the cell walls. Conceptually, the fiber saturation point is defined as the moisture content at which cell walls are completely saturated (maximum amount of bound water) and no liquid water exists in the cell lumina; the fiber saturation point of wood averages approximately 30% MC but can vary by species and within individual pieces of wood. Adhered wood products such as OSB are generally less hygroscopic than solid wood (Carll and Wiedenhoeft 2009) and thus have lower fiber saturation points. This is a result of the manufacturing process, which involves high temperature and pressure, and a result of the fact that OSB includes non-hygroscopic resins and wax.

Below the fiber saturation point, moisture content of wood depends on the relative humidity (RH) and temperature of the surrounding air. Equilibrium moisture content (EMC) at a given temperature and RH is defined as that moisture content at which wood is neither gaining nor losing moisture. The relationship between EMC and relative humidity at constant temperature is referred to as a sorption isotherm. The history of a wood specimen also affects its EMC; this is called sorption hysteresis. The EMC at a particular RH is higher when equilibrium is reached from a prior wet condition (desorption) than when reached from a prior dry condition (adsorption). However, this phenomenon is commonly neglected in many hygrothermal analyses. For this study, an average of the adsorption and desorption curves is used. Figure 1 shows an average sorption isotherm for solid wood and for OSB at room temperature.

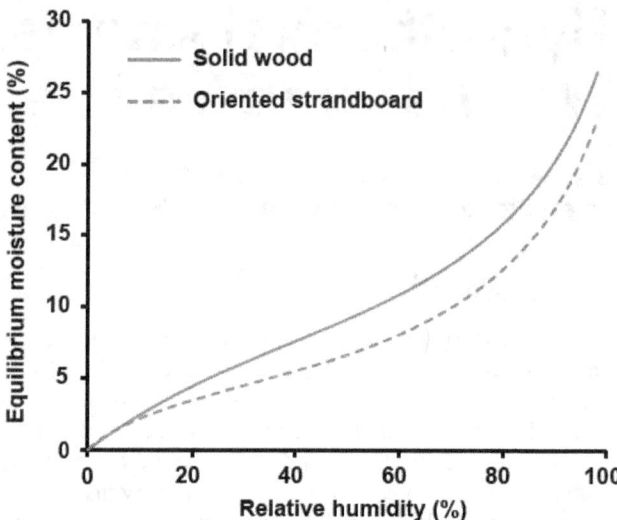

Figure 1. Sorption isotherms for solid wood and oriented strandboard (OSB) at room temperature. The curve for solid wood is based on the *Wood Handbook* (Glass and Zelinka 2010). The curve for OSB is based on a fit to data compiled from Richards et al. (1992); Kumaran (2001); Kumaran et al. (2002); Ojanen et al. (2006); and Hartley et al. (2007).

The term "condensation" is commonly used in the construction industry and the building science community in a broad sense (see the discussion regarding the dew point method in Section 1.4). Strictly speaking, condensation is the change in phase from vapor to liquid. The change from the vapor phase to the adsorbed phase (bound water) is known as sorption. Capillary condensation may occur in small pores in wood at very high relative humidity levels. The general term "moisture accumulation" is preferred to describe an increase in moisture content either from sorption or capillary condensation (in either the hygroscopic or over-hygroscopic range).

1.3 Moisture Performance Thresholds

A detailed overview of failure criteria for building materials is given by Viitanen and Salonvaara (2001). Potential issues relevant to wall structural sheathing are wood decay, mold growth, corrosion of metal fasteners, expansion/contraction damage, and loss of structural capacity. It is commonly held that the moisture content of wood needs to exceed the fiber saturation point for decay fungi to initiate propagation, while at levels below 20% MC their propagation is completely inhibited. The growth of decay fungi in wood also requires favorable temperature (approximately 5 to 40 °C). The traditional guideline for protection of wood and wood products from decay has been to keep the moisture content below 20% (Carll and Highley 1999). Although molds require a temperature range similar to that of decay fungi, they can propagate on surfaces without free water, provided the surface RH remains elevated. For protection of hygroscopic surfaces against mold propagation,

International Energy Agency (IEA) Annex 14 recommended that the surface relative humidity be kept below 80% RH on a monthly mean basis (Hens 1990). A similar criterion for minimizing mold growth was adopted by ASHRAE Standard 160 (ASHRAE 2009a): a 30-day running average surface RH < 80% when the 30-day running average surface temperature is between 5 and 40 °C. This RH level corresponds to an equilibrium MC of about 16% for solid wood and about 13% for OSB (see Fig. 1). Corrosion of metal fasteners can occur when moisture content exceeds 18% to 20% (Dennis et al. 1995). Expansion/contraction damage depends on the magnitude of the change in moisture content and the sensitivity of the particular wood product to such changes. Structural capacity generally decreases as moisture content increases. When wood products are used in conditions where moisture contents exceed 19% for solid wood or 16% for engineered wood products (including OSB), structural design standards require that wet service factors be applied because of reduced strength and stiffness. Performance thresholds for OSB are further discussed by Drumheller and Carll (2010).

This information is provided as a frame of reference. The purpose of this analysis is to compare the moisture performance of different wall constructions and to examine how their performance depends on certain environmental and material parameters. As discussed by Viitanen and Salonvaara (2001), failure predictions generally include a high degree of uncertainty because material properties may vary widely, boundary conditions cannot always be known with satisfactory accuracy, and degradation mechanisms have their own statistical variability that is then coupled with the uncertainty in the simulated temperature and moisture conditions. Pass/fail criteria are therefore not assigned in this study. However, the various performance metrics evaluated in this study do indeed allow for relative comparison of the different wood-frame wall assemblies.

1.4 Methods of Hygrothermal Analysis

Heat, air, and moisture (HAM) analysis methods can range widely in terms of the physical phenomena that they include (ASHRAE 2009b; Straube and Burnett 2001). On one end of the spectrum are simple steady-state models that include only heat conduction and vapor diffusion with constant material properties; on the other end are comprehensive computer models that include transient heat, vapor, liquid, and air transfer in as many as three dimensions, with variable material properties and detailed descriptions of phenomena such as airflow and wind-driven rain.

The traditional dew point method and its limitations are described in the ASHRAE Handbook of Fundamentals (ASHRAE 2009b) and TenWolde and Bomberg (2009). For a given indoor and outdoor temperature (typically monthly or seasonal mean values), the temperatures at each material interface within an assembly are calculated based on

steady-state heat flow using thermal resistance values of each material. The corresponding saturation vapor pressures can then be calculated. Vapor pressures are calculated at each material interface based on steady-state vapor diffusion, indoor and outdoor vapor pressures, and vapor permeance values of each material. If the vapor pressure exceeds the saturation vapor pressure at any location, then this condition is called "condensation."

The dew point method has many significant limitations. Moisture storage in hygroscopic materials is neglected, and all moisture transfer mechanisms other than vapor diffusion are excluded (air movement, liquid water flow, wind-driven rain, solar effects). The dependence of vapor permeance values on relative humidity is neglected. As noted by TenWolde and Bomberg (2009), the focus of this method is restricted to prevention of sustained surface condensation; many building failures, such as mold and mildew, buckling of siding, or paint failure, are not necessarily related to surface condensation. Conversely, some materials can tolerate limited "condensation," depending on the temperature conditions and the drying capability.

Over the past three decades, many detailed computer models have been developed to simulate temperature and moisture conditions in building envelope assemblies over time. Hens (1996) describes the general principles of hygrothermal analysis and provides details on models used in IEA Annex 24. Further information on some advanced hygrothermal models can be found in ASTM Manual 40 (Trechsel 2001). Recent work within IEA Annex 41 has led to the development of whole-building HAM models (Woloszyn and Rode 2008).

This study focuses on comparing the moisture performance of various wood-frame wall assemblies. For this application, a transient one-dimensional model with an hourly time step is sufficient. Software used in this study is Wärme und Feuchte instationär (WUFI, Transient Heat and Moisture) developed by the Fraunhofer Institute for Building Physics (IBP 2011). This hygrothermal model can account for the following phenomena:

- Heat capacity and heat transfer, including effects of phase change

- Moisture storage and moisture transfer, including vapor diffusion and liquid flow

- Material properties as a function of moisture content and temperature

- Boundary conditions including indoor temperature and humidity, outdoor temperature, humidity, solar radiation, cloud cover, wind speed and direction, rainfall, and wind-driven rain

- Wind-driven rain penetration at a specified material layer

- Moisture accumulation from air exfiltration at a specified material layer

Further information regarding the model can be found in Künzel (1995) and Trechsel (2001).

Air leakage through insulated building envelope assemblies is recognized as an important moisture transfer mechanism, especially for lightweight wood-frame cavities with low-density insulation (Straube and Burnett 2001, 2005; Glass and TenWolde 2007). Simulating air leakage in a realistic manner is difficult because the flow paths through building envelope assemblies are three-dimensional and difficult to define. Nevertheless, a number of studies have used one- and two-dimensional models to investigate moisture accumulation from air leakage (see, for example, Ojanen and Kumaran 1992, 1996; Burch and TenWolde 1993; Hagentoft and Harderup 1996; Kalamees and Kurnitski 2010). For one-dimensional models, air leakage is assumed to occur uniformly; however, measurements indicate that air leakage can be concentrated at specific sites, where moisture accumulation is likely to be higher (Tsongas and Nelson 1991). Nevertheless, a one-dimensional air exfiltration model is useful for comparing relative performance of different wall assemblies.

2. Goals and Objectives

This study investigates the moisture performance of 10 different residential wood-frame wall assemblies in a mixed-humid climate. The walls differ in stud cavity thickness, level of thermal insulation, presence and type of exterior insulation, and use of a Class II (0.1–1 perm) versus Class III (1–10 perm) interior vapor retarder. All walls include OSB sheathing, which serves as a common location for drawing comparisons. The goals of this study are to gain insight into how these wall assemblies respond to hygrothermal loads, to identify which components of the assembly have the greatest influence on moisture performance, and to identify potential moisture performance problems. The performance of the walls is compared in four important respects. First, seasonal trends in moisture, humidity, and temperature conditions are investigated, and the potential for wintertime moisture accumulation in OSB sheathing from vapor diffusion is assessed. Second, the rate at which OSB sheathing is able to dry from a high initial moisture content is compared. Drying capability is important because there is a good chance that wall assemblies will get wet at some time during their service life. Both the drying performance and seasonal trends include a sensitivity analysis to gauge the extent to which simulation results depend on varying the input parameters. Third, the effect of wind-driven rain intrusion on OSB moisture content is examined. Finally, the extent to which air exfiltration contributes to wintertime moisture accumulation in OSB is investigated.

The objectives of the study are as follows:

- Rank the various wall constructions in terms of minimizing the potential for moisture accumulation in the OSB sheathing by vapor diffusion and by air leakage

- Determine whether wintertime moisture accumulation differs in walls with 140-mm- (5.5-in.-) thick cavity insulation relative to walls with 89-mm- (3.5-in-) thick cavity insulation

- Determine the extent to which wintertime moisture accumulation in OSB sheathing depends on the vapor permeance of the interior vapor retarder

- Determine the effects of exterior insulation on moisture accumulation in OSB resulting from vapor diffusion and air leakage

- Rank the wall assemblies in terms of the drying capability of the OSB sheathing

- Determine critical parameters that affect drying rates

- Determine whether rigid insulation placed to the exterior of the OSB reduces the OSB drying rate

- Determine whether the presence of a kraft vapor retarder reduces the OSB drying rate

- Rank the wall assemblies in terms of their response to wind-driven rain penetration

3. Modeling Approach and Input Parameters

Simulations were run using WUFI® Pro 5.1 software for one-dimensional transient heat and moisture transfer (IBP 2011). Model input parameters include the following:

- Wall construction, geometry of components, and material properties of each component

- Moisture sources such as wind-driven rain or air exfiltration

- Wind-driven rain exposure

- Wall orientation

- Surface heat and mass transfer coefficients

- Initial temperature and moisture content in each component

- Calculation period (start and end dates and time step)

- Numerical calculation parameters

- Outdoor climate

- Indoor environment

Default values were selected for surface heat and mass transfer coefficients and numerical calculation parameters.

Table 1. Wall assembly insulation details

Wall	Abbreviation	Framing[a]	Insulation
1	R13 KFB	2 by 4	R-13 kraft-faced batt
2	R19 KFB	2 by 6	R-19 kraft-faced batt
3	R13 UFB	2 by 4	R-13 unfaced batt
4	R19 UFB	2 by 6	R-19 unfaced batt
5	R23 BIBS	2 by 6	R-23 blow-in blanket system[b]
6	R13 KFB + R5 XPS	2 by 4	R-13 kraft-faced batt in cavity plus exterior R-5 extruded polystyrene
7	R19 KFB + R5 XPS	2 by 6	R-19 kraft-faced batt in cavity plus exterior R-5 extruded polystyrene
8	R13 UFB + R5 XPS	2 by 4	R-13 unfaced batt in cavity plus exterior R-5 extruded polystyrene
9	R13 UFB + R10 XPS	2 by 4	R-13 unfaced batt in cavity plus exterior R-10 extruded polystyrene
10	R13 KFB + R5 MFI	2 by 4	R-13 kraft-faced batt in cavity plus exterior R-5 mineral fiber insulation

[a] Framing dimensions are nominal values in inches. Note that framing is not modeled; the model is one dimensional and includes a slice through the insulated cavity rather than the framing.

[b] The vapor diffusion resistance of the non-woven fabric in the blow-in blanket system is assumed to be negligible.

Convergence failures were eliminated by selecting a fine numerical grid and adaptive time step control. Other inputs are described below. Many of these refer to ASHRAE Standard 160 (ASHRAE 2009a). A sensitivity analysis was conducted with three of the wall assemblies to determine the extent to which simulation results depend on certain input parameters.

3.1 Wall Assemblies

All wall assemblies were simulated as having been constructed with wood framing, either standard 38 by 89 mm (nominal 2 by 4 in.) or standard 38 by 140 mm (nominal 2 by 6 in.). Wood framing was not modeled; the model is one dimensional and includes a section through the insulated cavity rather than the framing. All wall assemblies had an interior finish of 12.5-mm (½-in.) gypsum board, one coat of latex primer, and one coat of latex paint. The primer and paint were not modeled as separate layers; instead, an interior surface diffusion resistance was specified to correspond with the desired vapor permeance. Exterior structural sheathing in all wall assemblies was 11 mm (7/16 in.) OSB. In most cases, the water-resistive barrier (WRB) was a spun-bonded polyolefin (SBPO) membrane; however, for walls with extruded polystyrene (XPS) insulation, this membrane was omitted (in some cases XPS with taped seams qualifies as a WRB; for the purpose of hygrothermal simulation, it makes no difference whether an SBPO membrane is present in walls with exterior XPS). In the wall with exterior mineral fiber insulation (MFI), the SBPO membrane was placed between the OSB and the MFI. All wall assemblies were clad with vinyl siding. Table 1 summarizes the differences between the various wall assemblies.

3.2 Material Properties

Nominal thermal resistances (R-values) are expressed in this report in units of h·ft^2·°F·Btu^{-1}. In the simulations, thermal conductivity values have a default temperature coefficient of 2×10^{-4} W·m^{-1}·K^{-2}; thermal conductivity values were equated to values calculated from thickness and nominal R-values at a temperature of 24 °C (75 °F).

The vapor permeance values of certain materials were expected to strongly influence the simulation results. The key materials are described below. Vapor permeance values are given in units of U.S. perms. One perm is equivalent to 1 grain·ft^{-2}·h^{-1}·(in Hg)$^{-1}$. At 23 °C where laboratory permeance measurements are typically performed, 1 perm = 57.45 ng·m^{-2}·s^{-1}·Pa^{-1} (Thompson and Taylor 2008; note that the conversion from in Hg to Pa is temperature dependent). Simulations were performed in the SI unit system, and values were entered either as vapor diffusion resistance factor or as s_d value (the thickness of a still air layer with permeance equivalent to that of the material of given thickness). For conversions, a value of 190 ng·m^{-1}·s^{-1}·Pa^{-1} was used for the vapor permeability of still air.

3.2.1 Latex Primer and Paint on Interior Gypsum Board

Literature vapor permeance values show considerable variation, indicating that this parameter is important to include in the model sensitivity analysis. At the low end, the ASHRAE Handbook of Fundamentals (ASHRAE 2009c) lists values between 6 and 9 perms. ASHRAE Research Project 1018 (Kumaran et al. 2002) gives the permeance of gypsum board with one coat of primer and two coats of latex paint as a function of relative humidity (RH); values in the 40% to 60% RH range, typical of indoor conditions, are between 5 and 12 perms. Other studies have measured dry cup values of 16 to 40 perms for gypsum board with two coats of latex paint (Martin and Verschoor 1994; MHRA 2000; NAHBRC 2010). 10 perms was selected as the default value, and in the sensitivity analysis, the vapor permeance of the primer/paint layer was varied with values of 5 and 20 perms.

3.2.2 Asphalt-Coated Kraft Paper Facing on Batt Insulation

Measured values generally show an increase in permeance with increasing RH. The vapor permeance for this study was a user-defined function of RH based on literature data, as shown in Figure 2. Three design curves are shown. The "default" curve follows data from Burch et al. (1992).

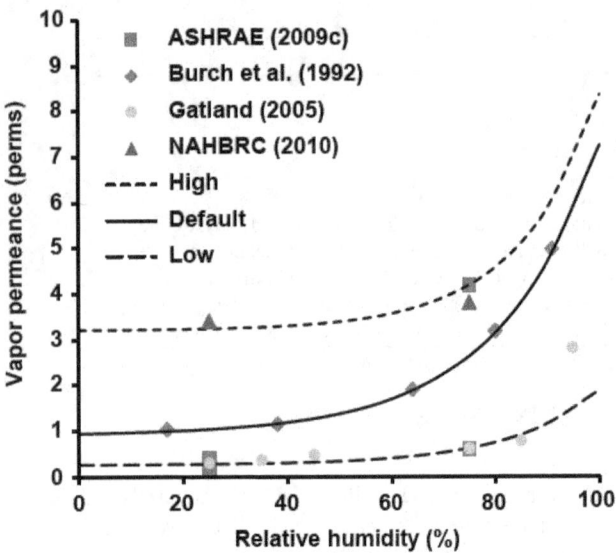

Figure 2. Data and design curves for water vapor permeance of asphalt-coated kraft paper as a function of relative humidity.

The "high" curve is an attempt to fit data at the higher end (ASHRAE 2009c, NAHBRC 2010). The "low" curve is an attempt to fit data at the lower end (ASHRAE 2009c; Gatland 2005).

3.2.3 Oriented Strandboard

The properties of OSB (with density of 650 kg·m^{-3}) from the WUFI Generic North America Database were used in the simulations. The vapor permeance at a thickness of 11 mm as a function of RH is shown as the default curve in Figure 3. This curve is reportedly taken from the measurements of Kumaran et al. (2002); it may be an average of the three different OSBs. It should be noted that WUFI includes simulation of liquid water transport at RH values above 80% in addition to vapor diffusion with RH-dependent vapor permeance. Figure 3 also shows other literature data (Dahl et al. 1996; Karagiozis and Wilkes 2004; Kumaran 2001; NAHBRC 2010; Ojanen et al. 2006; Timusk et al. 2009). These data were fit using a nonlinear least squares method; the best fit was found to agree well with the default curve. The "low" and "high" curves are the default curve scaled by factors of ½ and 2, respectively.

3.2.4 Spun-Bonded Polyolefin Membrane

The default vapor permeance was 50 perms, independent of RH (taken from the WUFI Generic North America Database). Other measured values range from 16 perms to approximately 120 perms (Kumaran 2001; Kumaran et al. 2002; NAHBRC 2010). In the sensitivity analysis, the vapor permeance was varied by factors of ½ (25 perms) and 2 (100 perms).

3.2.5 Extruded Polystyrene Rigid Insulation

The default vapor permeance was 0.76 perms for 25 mm (1 in., R-5) thickness, independent of RH (taken from the WUFI Generic North America Database). Kumaran (1996, 2001) lists values ranging from 0.65 perms to 1.4 perms. Kumaran et al. (2002) give a value of 0.84 perms. Manufacturer product literature gives a value of 1.1 perms. In the sensitivity analysis, a value of 1.4 perms was included in addition to the default value.

3.2.6 Rigid Mineral Fiber Insulation

The MFI product selected from the WUFI material database had a density of 87 kg·m^{-3} and a thermal conductivity of 0.035 W·m^{-1}·K^{-1} at 24 °C. A thickness of 31 mm (1.2 in.) was selected to achieve a thermal resistance of 0.88 m^2·K·W^{-1} (R-5). The vapor permeance at this thickness was 89 perms.

3.2.7 Vinyl Siding

An "equivalent vapor permeance" was used for vinyl siding. This is a method of modeling a cladding that is vapor impermeable but is back-ventilated by airflow. Values of 40 perms (BSC 2010b) and 70 perms (BSC 2010a) have been recommended. The default value used was 40 perms. In the sensitivity analysis, the vapor permeance was varied by factors of ½ (20 perms) and 2 (80 perms). The alternative, which is modeling an air space between the siding and house wrap, requires the selection of an air change rate. This air change rate is currently not well defined, and determining proper values is beyond the scope of this study.

3.3 Wind-Driven Rain

The default mode for simulations in this study was not to include wind-driven rain (WDR) intrusion. The ASHRAE Standard 160 calculation method prescribes that 1% of the wind-driven rain that reaches the wall is deposited on the exterior side of the WRB. However, this presents a problem when the WRB has no moisture storage capacity (as is the case for SBPO). An alternative approach is to introduce an additional layer in the wall assembly on the exterior side of the WRB to provide moisture storage capacity for the WDR that penetrates the cladding. This method has been used, for example, by Tariku et al. (2007). In this study, additional moisture storage layers in the assemblies were not included, and wind-driven rain was excluded from the simulations with the exception of Section 4.3.

The sensitivity of the wall assemblies to wind-driven rain intrusion directly into the OSB layer is examined in Section 4.3. Note that placing the penetrating rain at this location is an excursion from ASHRAE Standard 160. The calculation method used the following equation:

$$r_{bv} = F_E \cdot F_D \cdot F_L \cdot U \cdot \cos\theta \cdot r_h \qquad (1)$$

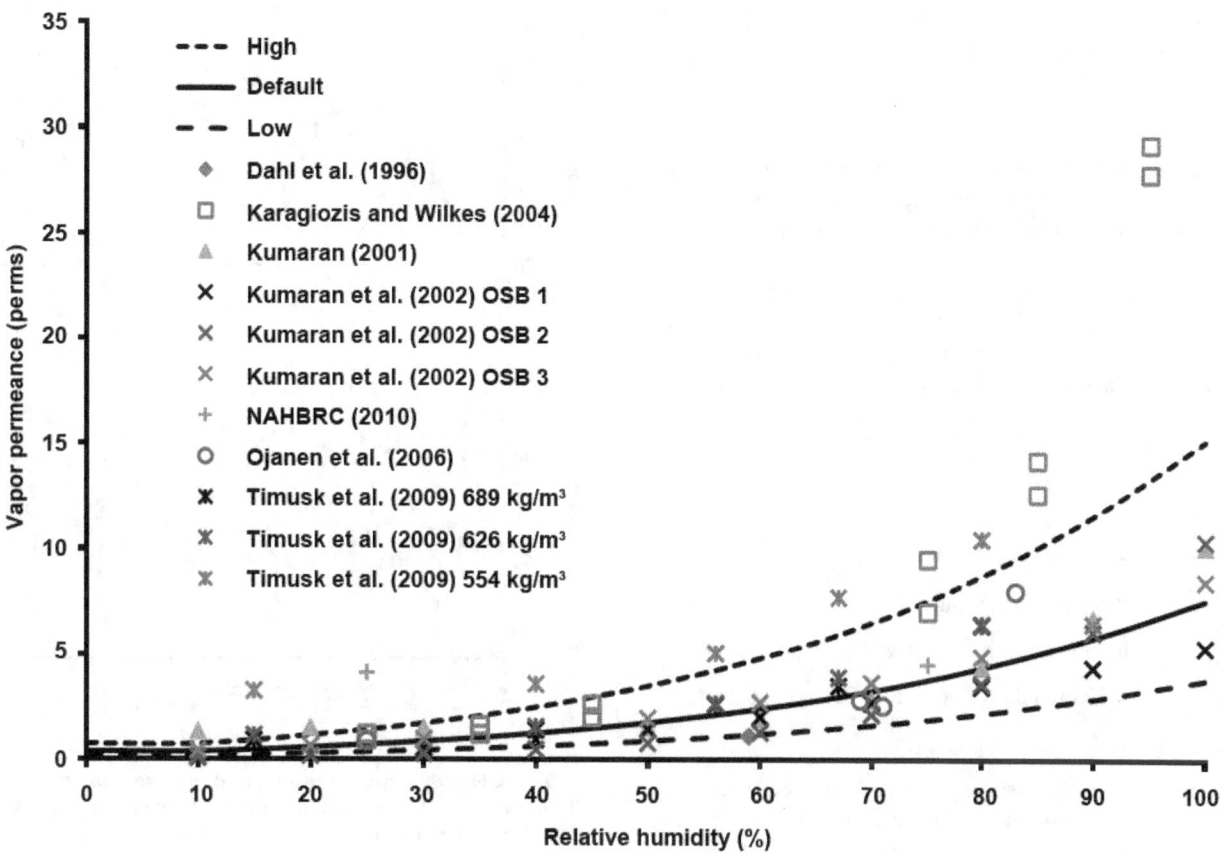

Figure 3. Data and design curves for vapor permeance of OSB at 11-mm thickness as a function of relative humidity.

where

r_{bv} is rain deposition on vertical wall (kg·m^{-2}·h^{-1})

F_E rain exposure factor

F_D rain deposition factor

F_L empirical constant (0.2 kg·s·m^{-3}·mm^{-1})

U hourly average wind speed at 10 m height (m·s^{-1})

θ angle between wind direction and normal to the wall

r_h rainfall intensity, horizontal surface (mm·h^{-1})

Wind speed, wind direction, and horizontal rainfall were taken from the outdoor climate file. ASHRAE Standard 160 rain exposure and deposition factors were selected: $F_E = 1.3$ is recommended for buildings up to 15 m (50 ft) on severe terrain; $F_D = 0.35$ is recommended for buildings with steep slope roofs (typical for residential construction). Two cases were examined in which 0.5% and 1% of the wind-driven rain that reached the cladding was deposited uniformly in the OSB layer. Simulations were run for 3 to 5 years to ensure that the annual moisture trend was stable.

3.4 Air Exfiltration

Water vapor carried by exfiltrating air can be deposited on a cold surface within the wall cavity. This phenomenon was simulated by introducing a moisture source at the interior surface of the OSB sheathing, using the IBP Infiltration Model in WUFI (IBP 2011). This moisture source m (kg·m^{-2}·h^{-1}) was calculated as follows:

$$m = q\left(c_i - c_{\text{sat},T}\right) \qquad (2)$$

where

q is air flow through the component (m^3·m^{-2}·h^{-1})

c_i indoor water vapor concentration (kg·m^{-3})

$c_{\text{sat},T}$ water vapor concentration at saturation corresponding to the temperature at the deposition site (kg·m^{-3})

Equation (2) neglects thermal effects associated with air exfiltration and water vapor phase change. It also treats sorption as equivalent to condensation; it assumes that the location where water vapor is deposited is at 100% RH. Only wetting is modeled; convective drying is neglected.

The air flow rate was calculated as the product of a leakage coefficient k ($m^3 \cdot m^{-2} \cdot h^{-1} \cdot Pa^{-1}$) and a pressure difference ΔP (Pa):

$$q = k \cdot \Delta P \qquad (3)$$

The leakage coefficient is associated with the level of air-tightness of the construction. The IBP Infiltration Model in WUFI includes three default airtightness classes (A, B, C). For the simulations in this study, k values of 0.02 and 0.04 $m^3 \cdot m^{-2} \cdot h^{-1} \cdot Pa^{-1}$ were selected, which are three and six times leakier, respectively, than the least airtight class (C) of the default classes. Pressure differences were assumed to be driven by stack effect only, and were calculated as follows:

$$\Delta P = \rho_o \frac{T_i - T_o}{T_i} g \frac{H}{2} \qquad (4)$$

where

ρ_o is   density of outdoor air (1.3 $kg \cdot m^{-3}$)

T_i indoor air temperature (K)

T_o outdoor air temperature (K)

g gravitational acceleration (9.81 $m \cdot s^{-2}$)

H height of the building (m)

Equation (4) calculates the pressure difference at the top of the wall at the top floor of the building and assumes that the reference pressure (neutral pressure plane) is at half the building height. A building height of 5 m (two-story residential building) was selected. For the month of January, the average pressure difference was 2.8 Pa. Values were generally between 1.5 Pa and 3.5 Pa during winter.

As stated previously, this model assumes that air leakage has no effect on temperature. This is reasonable for small airflows, but higher airflows entail greater heat flux and can raise the sheathing temperature, thereby reducing the rate of moisture accumulation. For the conditions investigated here, airflows were less than 0.2 $m^3 \cdot m^{-2} \cdot h^{-1}$ (0.06 $L \cdot m^{-2} \cdot s^{-1}$), which is well below the point at which air leakage lowers the rate of moisture accumulation (Ojanen and Kumaran 1996). Therefore, the model assumptions are not unreasonable.

3.5 Wall Orientation

The north-facing orientation was selected as the default because it was expected to have the highest OSB moisture content in winter and the slowest drying rate. South-, east-, and west-facing orientations were also examined in the sensitivity analysis. In the analysis of summer inward vapor diffusion, the south-facing orientation was chosen.

3.6 Initial Conditions

The initial temperature in each component was set to 20 °C. For investigating drying rates from a high moisture content, the initial moisture content of OSB was set to two times

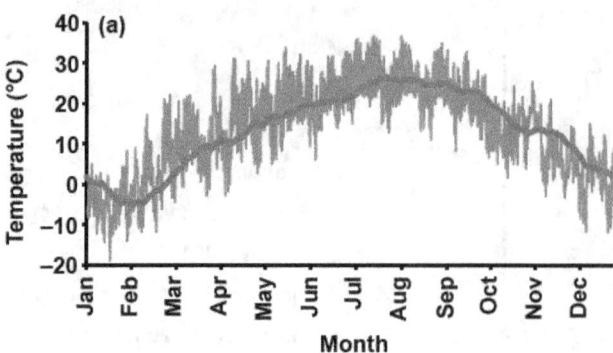

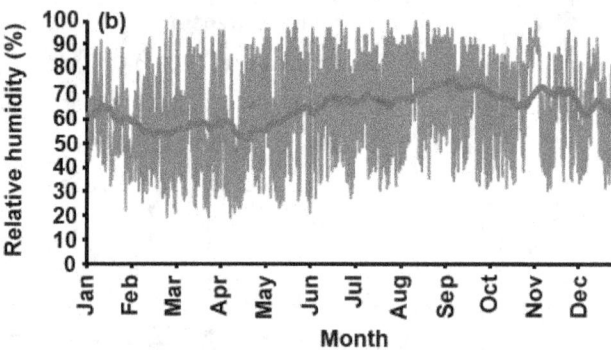

Figure 4. Hourly temperature (a) and relative humidity (b) conditions for the Baltimore warm year. Thick curves indicate 30-day running average values.

the equilibrium moisture content at 80% RH (at 20 °C), in accordance with ASHRAE Standard 160. This corresponds to 25.6% MC. For investigations other than drying performance, the initial conditions are not relevant; the simulations were run for multiple years to attain stable annual trends.

3.7 Calculation Period

Simulations were generally started on October 1 and ended 3 years later using a 1-h time step. In Section 4.2.1, simulations were started at different times of year to investigate the seasonal effect on drying performance.

3.8 Outdoor Climate

Simulations were run with both the "warm year" and "cold year" for Baltimore, Maryland. These correspond to the calendar years with third highest and third lowest annual average temperature out of 30 consecutive years (1961–1990). These are called "moisture design reference years" in ASHRAE Standard 160. Temperature and relative humidity conditions are depicted in Figures 4 and 5.

3.9 Indoor Environment

Indoor temperature and humidity conditions were sine curves as described below.

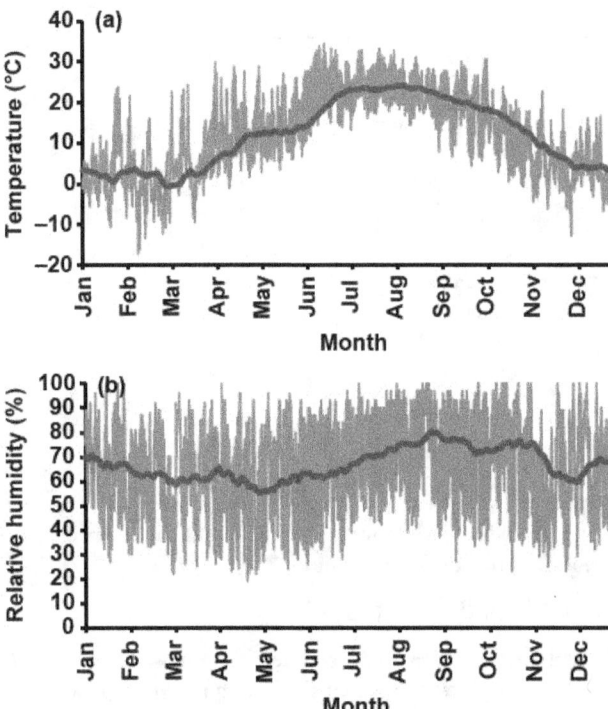

Figure 5. Hourly temperature (a) and relative humidity (b) conditions for the Baltimore cold year. Thick curves indicate 30-day running average values.

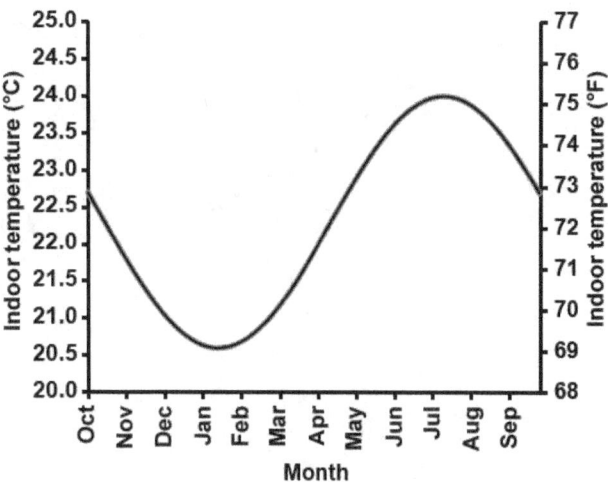

Figure 6. Indoor temperature conditions for simulations.

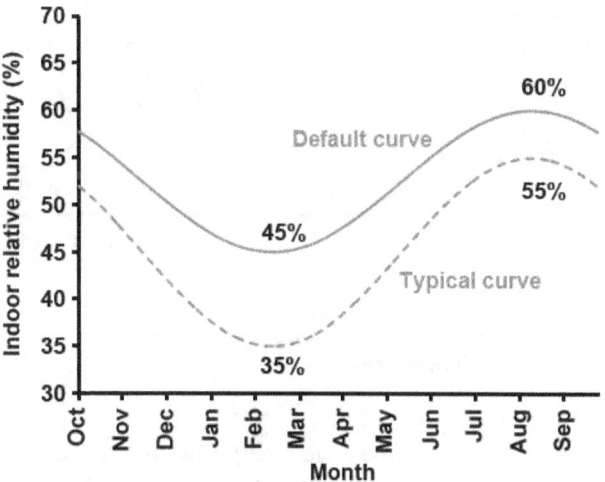

Figure 7. Indoor relative humidity conditions for simulations.

3.9.1 Indoor Temperature

The indoor temperature curve (Fig. 6) has a mean value of 22.3 °C (72.1 °F), a minimum of 20.6 °C (69.1 °F) on January 15, and a maximum of 24.0 °C (75.2 °F) on July 15. These values were based on recent measurements from a mixed-humid climate location, Knoxville, Tennessee (Antretter et al. 2010). These values also happen to be in relatively good agreement with the ASHRAE Standard 160 indoor design temperature, which defines a heating set point of 21.1 °C (70 °F) and a cooling set point of 23.9 °C (75 °F).

3.9.2 Indoor Humidity

The default indoor humidity curve (Fig. 7), which represents higher-than-average humidity levels (approximating 90th percentile values), has a minimum of 45% RH on February 15 and a maximum of 60% RH on August 15. For the sensitivity analysis, a second curve was used to represent typical (average) humidity levels. This curve has a minimum of 35% RH and a maximum of 55% RH.

The simulation results were expected to depend strongly on the winter indoor RH values. The values of 35% RH for "typical" and 45% RH for "default" were based on measurements in occupied houses in climate zone 4A (personal communication from J. Wiehagen, Energy Engineer, NAHB Research Center, February 2011). The following justification supports these selected values.

First, the typical winter minimum value (35% RH) is similar to measurements reporting a winter average of 40% RH for 10 houses in another mixed-humid location, Knoxville, Tennessee (Antretter et al. 2010). Knoxville is a slightly warmer climate, so the trend is in the right direction (lower RH in the colder location).

Second, the default winter minimum value (45% RH) is between the design values calculated according to the ASHRAE Standard 160 simplified and intermediate methods. In the simplified method, the indoor RH (at 70 °F) is calculated as a function of daily average outdoor temperature. Using instead the 1971–2000 monthly average outdoor temperatures for December, January, and February in Baltimore, the winter design indoor RH averaged over these months is 51% RH.

9

Table 2. Parameter values for sensitivity analysis

Wall assembly	Parameter	Default value	Alternatives	Reference
2. R19 KFB	Kraft vapor permeance	Default curve	Low, high	Figure 2
4. R19 UFB	Primer + paint vapor permeance	10 perms	5 perms, 20 perms	Section 3.2.1
	OSB[a] vapor permeance	Default curve	× ½, × 2	Figure 3
	SPBO[b] vapor permeance	50 perms	25 perms, 100 perms	Section 3.2.4
	Vinyl siding equivalent vapor permeance	40 perms	20 perms, 80 perms	Section 3.2.7
	Wall orientation	North	South, East, West	Section 3.5
	Indoor humidity	Default curve	Typical curve	Figure 7
8. R13 UFB + R5 XPS	XPS[c] vapor permeance	0.76 perms	1.4 perms	Section 3.2.5

[a]Oriented strandboard.
[b]Spun-bonded polyolefin membrane.
[c]Extruded polystyrene.

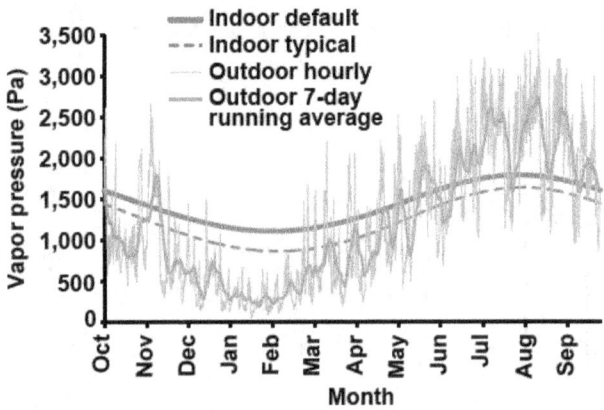

Figure 8. Indoor and outdoor vapor pressure conditions for simulations (Baltimore warm year).

The intermediate method calculates the indoor vapor pressure using a mass balance with inputs including outdoor vapor pressure, moisture generation rate, and ventilation rate (TenWolde and Walker 2001). The ASHRAE Standard 160 committee has recently approved Addendum b, which revises the residential moisture generation rates in the standard, as recent analysis suggested that these rates were too high (Glass and TenWolde 2009; TenWolde 2011). For a house with four bedrooms, a moisture generation rate of 11 kg·day^{-1} was selected (based on the value in the addendum versus the old value of 15 kg·day^{-1}). The default value of 0.2 air changes per hour was used, in conjunction with a building volume of 500 m^3 (17,700 ft^3, approximately the volume of a house with an area of 2,200 ft^2). Using 1971–2000 monthly average outdoor vapor pressures for December, January, and February in Baltimore, the winter design indoor humidity value averaged over these months is 44% RH.

Figure 8 compares indoor and outdoor vapor pressure conditions (calculated from temperature and RH). The outdoor vapor pressures are based on the Baltimore warm year. As

expected, indoor vapor pressure generally exceeds outdoor vapor pressure during late fall, winter, and early spring. The trend is opposite during summer.

3.10 Sensitivity Analysis

To determine which input parameters are most critical and to gauge the extent to which simulation results depend on varying the input parameters, a systematic sensitivity analysis was conducted that included several different wall constructions. Only one parameter was altered at a time while all the others were held at default values. The default parameters and alternatives are given in Table 2.

4. Results and Discussion

4.1 Vapor Diffusion Analysis: Seasonal OSB Moisture Content, Temperature, and Relative Humidity

This section discusses the seasonal vapor diffusion performance of the wall assemblies with a focus on wintertime moisture accumulation in OSB sheathing. Summertime inward vapor diffusion is also considered. Wind-driven rain and air exfiltration are not included here; the effects of these phenomena are considered in Sections 4.3 and 4.4.

4.1.1 Wintertime OSB Moisture Content

Simulations for each wall assembly were run for 3 years. The OSB moisture content during the second and third years was nearly identical indicating stable annual cycles. Figures in this section show the third year of the simulation.

Figure 9 shows the daily average OSB moisture content (the ratio of mass of moisture to mass of dry material expressed as a percentage, averaged over the thickness of the OSB layer) over a year starting October 1 for Wall 3 with unfaced batt insulation (R13 UFB). The figure indicates that OSB reaches a higher moisture content when simulated with the Baltimore warm year than with the cold year. This trend is found for all 10 walls. This peculiar result happens because

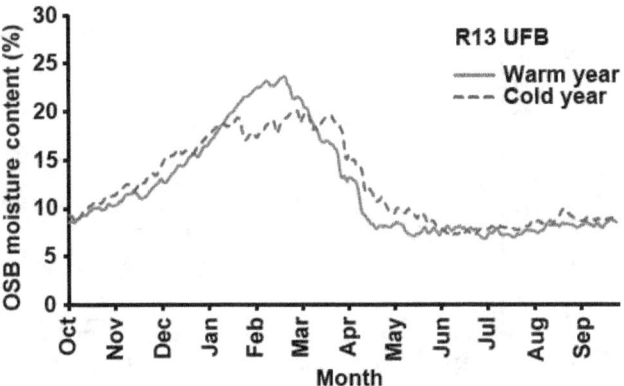

Figure 9. OSB moisture content in Wall 3 (R13 UFB) for one year simulation using Baltimore warm and cold years.

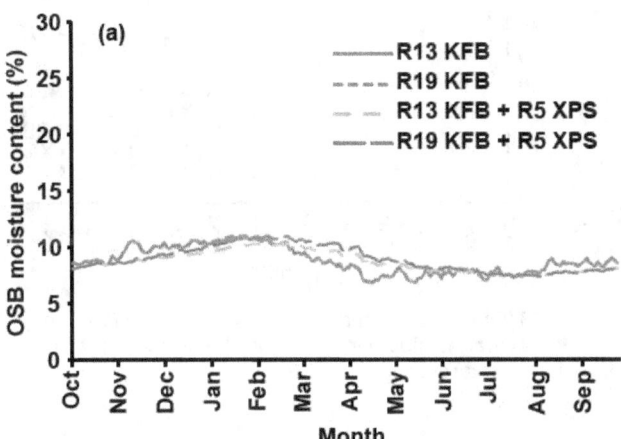

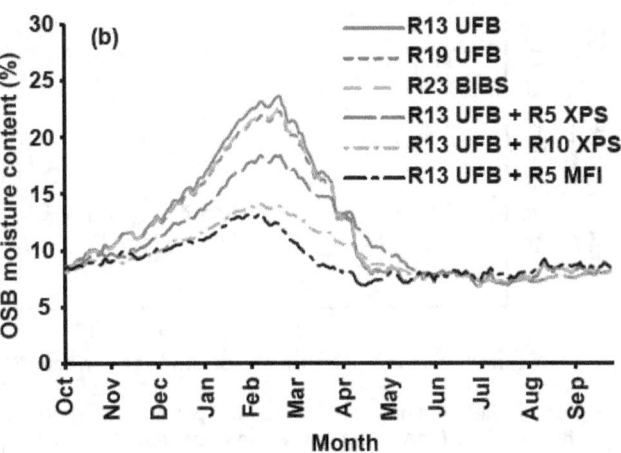

Figure 10. OSB moisture content in walls with (a) and without (b) a kraft vapor retarder.

the 10th percentile warm and cold years are selected based on annual average temperature. The "warm" year actually has a colder winter than the "cold" year. The warm year is used in subsequent simulations.

Figure 10a compares seasonal trends in the four walls having a kraft vapor retarder. The annual variation in moisture content is small, with values reaching approximately 11% in winter and approximately 7% in summer. Wintertime MC values are slightly higher for walls with R-19 cavity insulation than their R-13 counterparts; this difference is more pronounced for the walls with exterior XPS insulation. The slight differences in OSB moisture content for walls of differing thickness stem from differences in temperature of OSB during winter, as discussed later.

In contrast, wall assemblies without a kraft vapor retarder reach much higher OSB moisture contents during winter, as shown in Figure 10b. Peak values range from about 13% in Wall 10 (R13 UFB + R5 MFI) to about 24% in Wall 3 (R13 UFB). Walls 4 (R19 UFB) and 5 (R23 BIBS) are nearly identical. In this analysis that considers only vapor diffusion, a kraft vapor retarder has a greater effect on keeping OSB dry than exterior insulation. This finding could have been predicted from a simple dew point method calculation.

The walls with exterior insulation (without a kraft vapor retarder) accumulate less moisture in the OSB than the R13 UFB reference wall, as a result of the OSB temperature being higher. Two effects are apparent. First, OSB moisture content is considerably lower with R10 XPS than with R5 XPS, consistent with the OSB being warmer with R10 XPS; warmer OSB tends to stay drier. Second, OSB moisture content is considerably lower with R5 mineral fiber insulation than with R5 extruded polystyrene. This difference occurs because MFI is vapor permeable, allowing water vapor to pass through the OSB to the exterior, whereas XPS is vapor impermeable, impeding outward drying of the OSB.

4.1.2 Wintertime Temperature and Relative Humidity

Figures 11a and 11b compare temperatures at the interior surface of the OSB for walls with and without a kraft vapor retarder. 30-day running average values are depicted for ease of comparison (hourly or daily average values fluctuate to a large degree, making visual comparison difficult). The kraft vapor retarder essentially has no effect on OSB temperature. As expected, the OSB is warmer during winter in walls with exterior insulation. R-5 XPS and R-5 MFI are practically identical, and R-10 XPS keeps the OSB warmer than R-5 XPS (Figure 11b). Walls with R-13 cavity insulation have slightly warmer OSB than otherwise identical walls with R-19 cavity insulation.

Figure 12 illustrates the effect of the kraft vapor retarder on the relative humidity at the interior surface of the OSB. Wall 3 (R13 UFB) has a much higher RH than Wall 1 (R13 KFB). Figures 13a and 13b show the relative humidity at the interior surface of the OSB for the same walls as depicted in Figures 11a and 11b, respectively (using 30-day running averages).

The relationship between wintertime relative humidity and temperature at the interior surface of the OSB is depicted

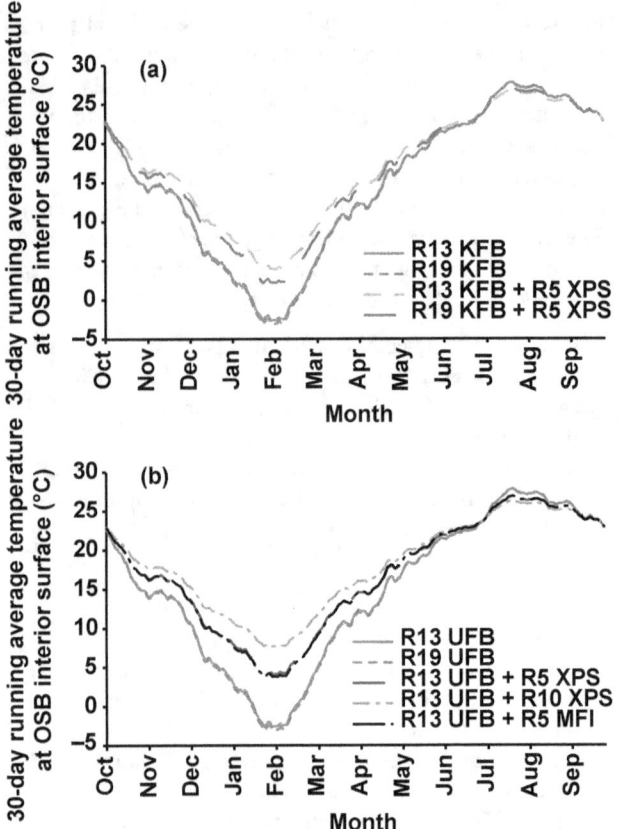

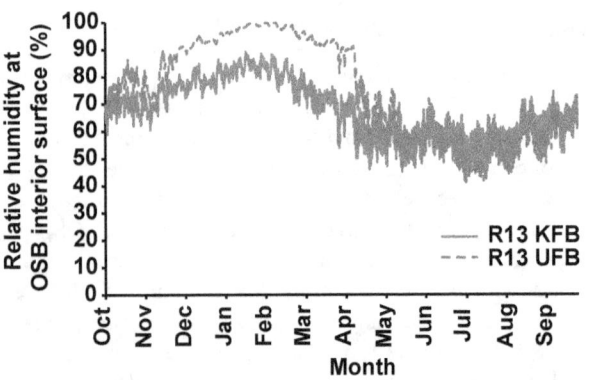

Figure 11. OSB interior surface temperatures (30-day running average values) in walls with (a) and without (b) a kraft vapor retarder.

Figure 12. Effect of kraft vapor retarder on OSB interior surface relative humidity (hourly values).

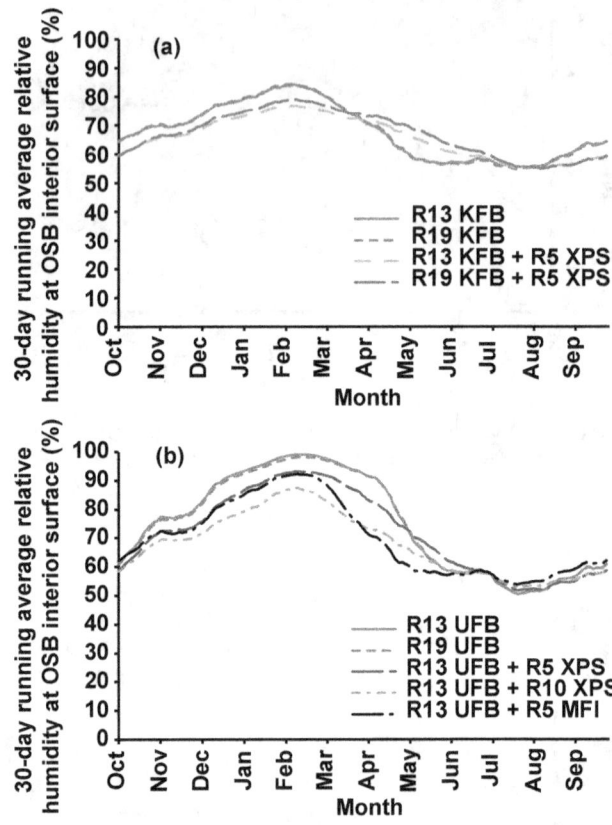

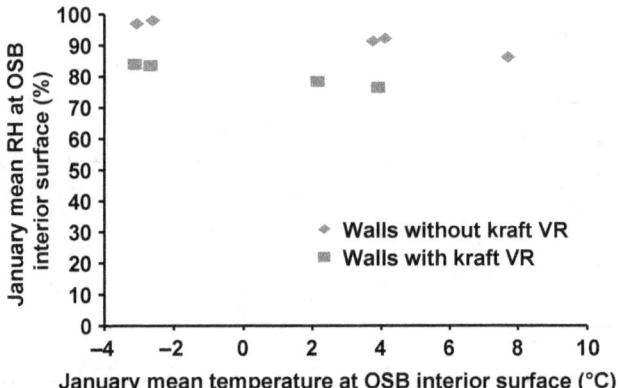

Figure 13. OSB interior surface relative humidity (30-day running average values) in walls with (a) and without (b) a kraft vapor retarder.

Figure 14. Relative humidity versus temperature at interior surface of OSB (January mean values) for walls with and without a kraft vapor retarder (VR).

in Figure 14, using January mean values. This figure indicates that surface RH generally decreases as temperature increases, and that RH is generally lower when a kraft vapor retarder is present. The trends in temperature and relative humidity are consistent with the trends in moisture content described above.

Further insight into the moisture dynamics of the different walls can be gained by looking at the relative humidity levels at various points through the OSB. Figure 15a shows 30-day running average RH values at the interior surface,

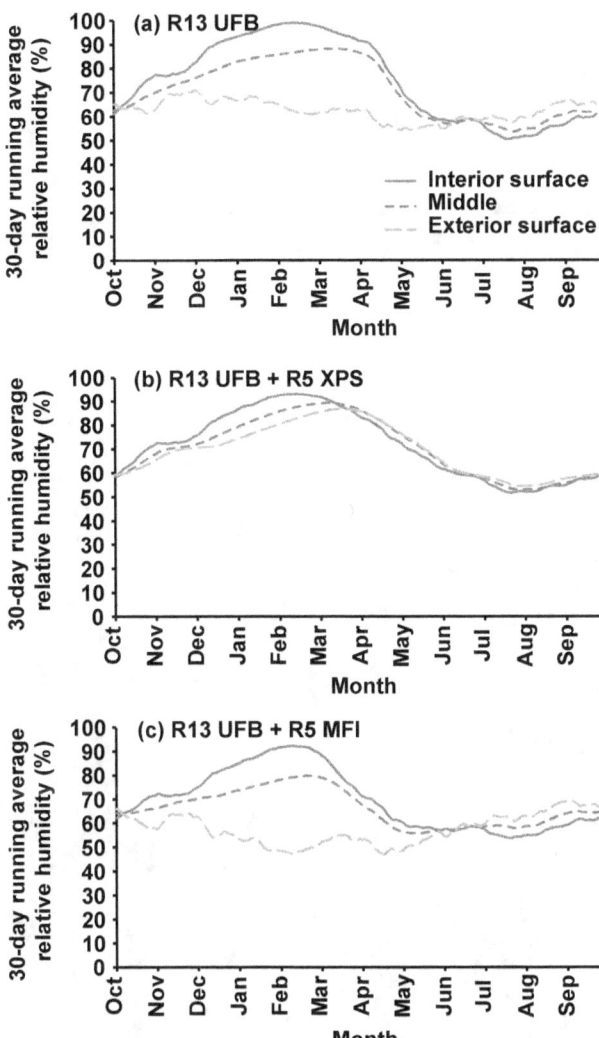

Figure 15. Relative humidity at interior surface, middle, and exterior surface of OSB (30-day running average values) for (a) Wall 3, R13 UFB; (b) Wall 8, R13 UFB + R5 XPS; and (c) Wall 10, R13 UFB + R5 MFI.

middle, and exterior surface of the OSB in wall 3 (R13 UFB). The temperature gradient across the OSB is negligible, so the RH values are approximately proportional to vapor pressure values. The RH at the interior surface exceeds 90% for much of the winter; there is a strong gradient from the interior to the exterior surface of the OSB. The OSB middle and interior surface dry below 70% RH by May, and in June the gradient is reversed (higher RH at the exterior).

Figure 15b shows the effect of adding exterior XPS. First the RH at the OSB interior surface is lower than in Figure 15a because of the temperature effect discussed above. Second, the RH at the exterior surface is elevated compared to Figure 15a. This occurs because the low-perm XPS reduces the rate at which moisture passes through the OSB when

the vapor drive is outward. The OSB dries more uniformly (smaller RH gradient) than in Figure 15a and at a slower rate, from March into July.

When XPS is replaced with MFI (Figure 15c), the temperature effect still lowers the RH at the OSB interior surface compared with Figure 15a. In contrast to XPS, the high vapor permeance of MFI in conjunction with the temperature effect results in lower RH at the OSB exterior surface compared with Figure 15a. Furthermore, the OSB middle and interior surface dry more quickly, falling below 70% RH by April.

4.1.3 Sensitivity of Wintertime OSB Moisture Content to Varying Parameters

This section examines the effects of varying different parameters on wintertime moisture performance of OSB sheathing based on vapor diffusion. Parameters were varied as described in Section 3.10.

Table 3 summarizes the influence of the different parameters, using maximum wintertime OSB moisture content as a metric. Many of the observed trends are expected; trends related to indoor humidity levels and vapor permeance of the various components could have been predicted from the dew point method.

OSB moisture content in Wall 2 (R19 KFB) is sensitive to the vapor permeance of the kraft facing: as expected, higher permeance corresponds with higher wintertime moisture content.

The following observations are made regarding OSB moisture content in Wall 4 (R19 UFB):

- Wintertime MC is highly sensitive to the vapor permeance of the latex primer/paint on the interior gypsum board. Higher permeance corresponds with higher moisture content, as more water vapor diffuses into the OSB.

- Wintertime MC is somewhat sensitive to the vapor permeance of the OSB itself. Higher permeance corresponds with lower moisture content, as moisture more readily diffuses through the OSB.

- Wintertime MC is relatively insensitive to the vapor permeance of the spun bonded polyolefin membrane and to the equivalent vapor permeance of the vinyl siding, both of which are much more permeable than OSB.

- Wintertime MC is highly sensitive to wall orientation. The north-facing wall (default) accumulates the most moisture; the east- and west-facing walls are nearly identical; and the south-facing wall accumulates the least moisture because of solar exposure.

- Wintertime MC is highly sensitive to indoor humidity levels. The higher (default) indoor humidity curve (Fig. 7) results in a greater degree of moisture accumulation than the typical indoor humidity curve.

Table 3. Summary of wintertime vapor diffusion sensitivity analysis

Wall assembly	Parameter	Value	Maximum OSB moisture content (kg·kg⁻¹)	Change from default (%)
R19 KFB		Default values	0.111	—
	Kraft vapor permeance	Low	0.104	− 6
		High	0.136	+ 22
R19 UFB		Default values	0.223	—
	Primer/paint vapor permeance	5 perms	0.175	− 22
		20 perms	0.268	+ 20
	OSB vapor permeance	×0.5	0.240	+ 8
		×2	0.199	− 11
	SBPO vapor permeance	25 perms	0.227	+ 2
		100 perms	0.221	− 1
	Vinyl siding equivalent vapor permeance	20 perms	0.228	+ 2
		80 perms	0.221	− 1
	Wall orientation	South	0.173	− 22
		East	0.209	− 6
		West	0.205	− 8
	Indoor humidity	Typical curve	0.164	− 26
R13 UFB + R5 XPS	XPS vapor Permeance	Default (0.76 perms)	0.184	—
		1.4 perms	0.174	− 5

OSB moisture content in Wall 8 (R13 UFB + R5 XPS) is slightly sensitive to the vapor permeance of the exterior extruded polystyrene insulation. Higher permeance corresponds with lower wintertime MC, as moisture diffuses more readily through the OSB and XPS. The vapor permeance of XPS is in a range similar to that of OSB (in contrast to SBPO for example), so it does make a difference.

Ranking the sensitivity of the maximum wintertime OSB moisture content, it is most sensitive to indoor humidity levels. Next, this metric is sensitive to kraft vapor permeance, wall orientation, and primer/paint vapor permeance to approximately the same extent. The maximum MC is somewhat sensitive to OSB vapor permeance and less so to XPS vapor permeance. It is rather insensitive to vinyl siding equivalent vapor permeance and SBPO vapor permeance.

4.1.4 Summertime Inward Vapor Diffusion

Inward vapor diffusion occurs during summer when outdoor vapor pressure exceeds indoor vapor pressure (Fig. 8). The inward vapor drive can be magnified when moisture stored in absorptive claddings, such as masonry, stucco, or adhered stone veneer, is warmed by solar radiation. This effect has been studied extensively with field testing, laboratory measurements, and modeling (Derome 2010). In this study, the cladding is vinyl siding, which is nonabsorptive and therefore does not amplify the inward vapor drive.

The location of interest in the wall assemblies is the exterior surface (cavity side) of the kraft vapor retarder because this layer limits inward drying. Less permeable vapor retarders, such as polyethylene, may experience condensation from summer inward vapor diffusion. Condensation would not be expected on kraft paper because it is hygroscopic and

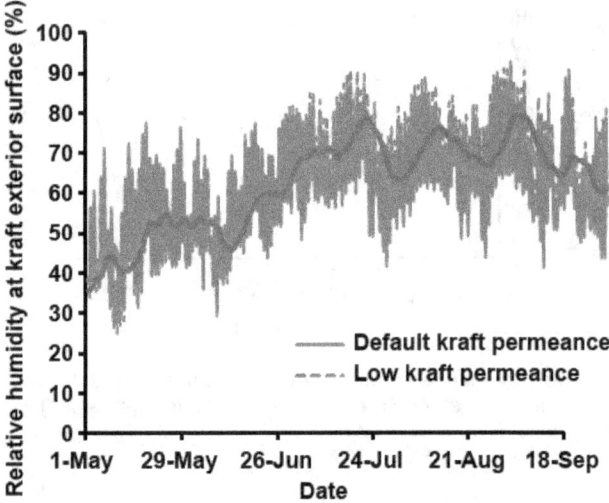

Figure 16. Effect of kraft vapor permeance on relative humidity levels at the cavity side of the kraft vapor retarder (Wall 1, R13 KFB). Hourly values and 7-day running average values are shown for each case.

because its vapor permeance increases considerably at high relative humidity (Fig. 2). However, sustained high RH could lead to mold growth. RH levels at the exterior surface of the kraft vapor retarder were therefore examined. Simulations were run for south-facing walls using the Baltimore warm year.

Figure 16 compares hourly RH values in Wall 1 (R13 KFB) using default and low kraft vapor permeance functions. As expected, RH values are higher when the vapor permeance

Table 4. Summertime relative humidity at exterior surface of kraft vapor retarder

Wall assembly	Maximum 30-day running average relative humidity (%)	
	Default kraft vapor permeance	Low kraft vapor permeance
1. R13 KFB	68.7	73.1
2. R19 KFB	68.8	72.9
6. R13 KFB + R5 XPS	63.6	64.7
7. R19 KFB + R5 XPS	64.5	65.1

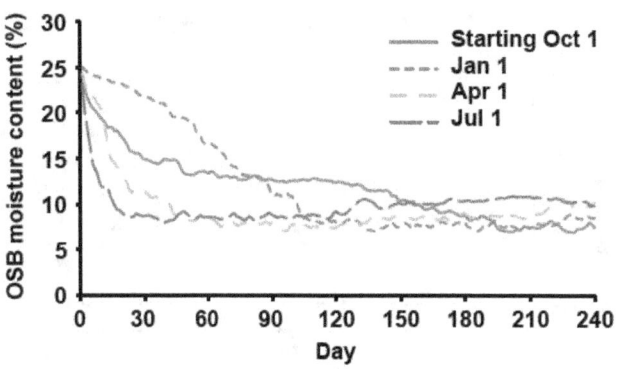

Figure 18. Effect of different starting dates on OSB drying performance in Wall 1 (R13 KFB).

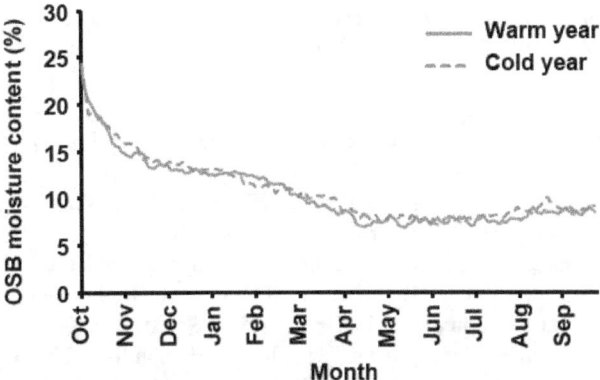

Figure 17. OSB moisture content in Wall 1 (R13 KFB) for one year simulation starting October 1 using Baltimore warm and cold years.

4.2 Drying Performance of OSB

4.2.1 Effect of Simulation Starting Date

Figure 17 shows the daily average OSB moisture content over a year starting October 1 for Wall 1 (R13 KFB). The initial moisture content is approximately 25%. The wall faces north, and the default input parameters given previously are used in simulations. There is little difference in performance between the warm and cold years, so from here on different wall constructions are compared using only the warm year.

Figure 18 depicts OSB moisture content for the same wall (R13 KFB) with simulations starting October 1, January 1, April 1, and July 1. The drying rate is fastest in July and slowest in January, as expected; drying normally occurs faster at higher temperatures.

is lower. Hourly values in some cases reach 93% RH, but 7-day running average values never exceed 80% RH. The maximum 30-day running average values are given in Table 4 for the walls with kraft vapor retarders. All values are well below the 80% threshold for mold growth (Section 1.3). Differences between R-13 and R-19 walls are minimal, but walls with exterior XPS insulation have somewhat lower RH than those without XPS because the low-perm XPS impedes inward vapor diffusion.

Table 5 summarizes the drying performance of all 10 wall assemblies. It lists the number of days it takes the OSB to dry below 16% MC (an arbitrary threshold for comparing relative performance). The wall assemblies can be grouped into four different classes:

Table 5. Number of days for OSB to dry below 16% MC from different starting dates

Wall assembly	Simulation starting date			
	October 1	January 1	April 1	July 1
1. R13 KFB	22	64	13	5
2. R19 KFB	21	62	13	5
3. R13 UFB	28	98	14	5
4. R19 UFB	25	90	13	5
5. R23 BIBS	28	91	13	5
6. R13 KFB + R5 XPS	203	136	59	29
7. R19 KFB + R5 XPS	205	137	56	20
8. R13 UFB + R5 XPS	202	125	42	18
9. R13 UFB + R10 XPS	167	111	43	22
10. R13 UFB + R5 MFI	22	66	14	9

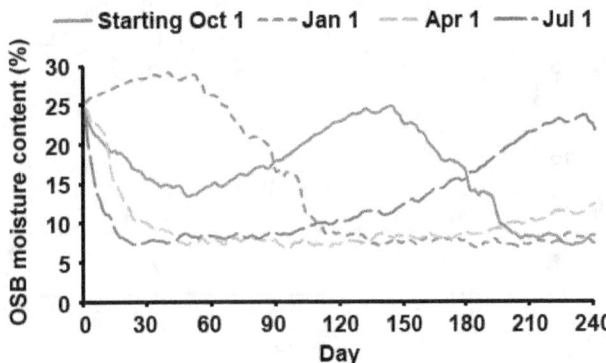

Figure 19. Effect of different starting dates on OSB drying performance in Wall 3 (R13 UFB).

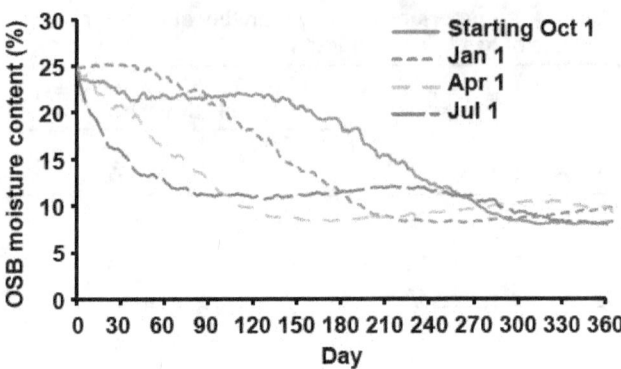

Figure 21. Effect of different starting dates on OSB moisture content in Wall 6 (R13 KFB + R5 XPS).

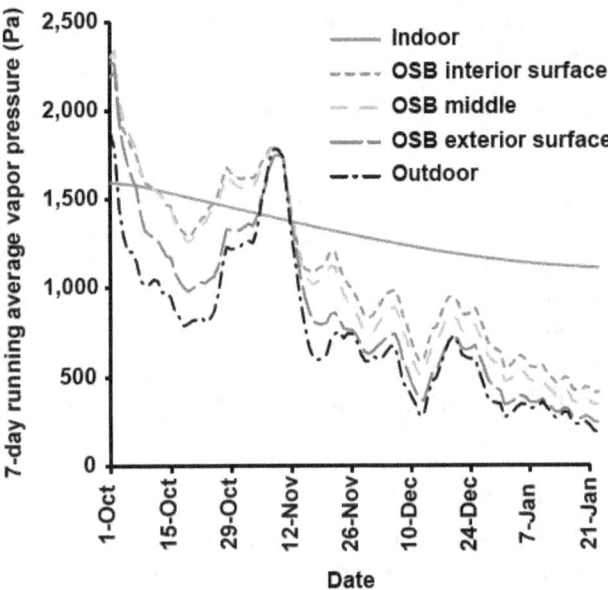

Figure 20. Vapor pressure conditions (7-day running average values) at indoor and outdoor boundaries and at interior, middle, and exterior of OSB in Wall 3 (R13 UFB).

1. Walls 1 and 2 (R13 KFB and R19 KFB) are practically identical in drying performance.

2. Walls 3–5 (R13 UFB, R19 UFB, and R23 BIBS) are slower to dry in fall and winter than Group 1, but are practically identical to Group 1 in spring and summer. These walls dry more slowly in fall and winter because of the interior humidity load, and they accumulate more moisture during cold weather (see Section 4.1). Figure 19 shows the wall with R13 UFB as an example of this group. Figure 20 depicts vapor pressure conditions indoors, outdoors, and at the interior and exterior surfaces of the OSB in the same wall starting October 1. This figure indicates that the exterior OSB surface dries more rapidly than the interior surface and that the vapor pressure gradient across the OSB is from interior to exterior.

3. Walls 6–9 with exterior XPS insulation dry much more slowly in all seasons than walls in Groups 1 and 2. Figure 21 shows Wall 6 (R13 KFB + R5 XPS) as an example of this group. The low-perm XPS greatly impedes outward drying of the OSB. In spring and summer, drying is generally faster in walls without a kraft vapor retarder (compare R13 UFB + R5 XPS with R13 KFB + R5 XPS). Drying is faster for R10 XPS than for R5 XPS in fall and winter because the temperature of the OSB is higher. However, this trend is reversed in summer; drying is faster for R5 XPS than for R10 XPS because R10 keeps the OSB cooler in summer and reduces heat flow to the OSB.

4. Wall 10 (R13 UFB + R5 MFI) is similar to Groups 1 and 2. The vapor permeable exterior insulation appears to have differing effects in cold weather and warm weather. This wall dries faster in fall and winter than Group 2 because the R5 MFI warms the OSB. However, in summer it dries slightly slower than Groups 1 and 2 because the exterior insulation keeps the OSB cooler and reduces heat flow to the OSB.

Comparisons from here on are drawn based on October 1 as the starting date. Figure 22a compares wall assemblies without exterior insulation (Walls 1–5). The differences in initial drying rate are minimal. The divergence in OSB moisture content in late November is evident between walls with and without a kraft vapor retarder. This reflects the wintertime trends discussed in Section 4.1.

Figure 22b compares OSB drying performance for walls with XPS or MFI exterior insulation. In all walls with R-5 XPS, drying below 20% MC does not occur until spring (note the different x-axis between Figures 22a and b). Increasing the R-value of XPS from 5 to 10 (with R-13 UFB) improves the drying rate. The most dramatic difference is between XPS and MFI (green and orange curves in Fig. 22b); permeable exterior insulation allows the OSB to dry much more rapidly. The same trend of faster drying with exterior MFI than with exterior XPS was found by Smegal

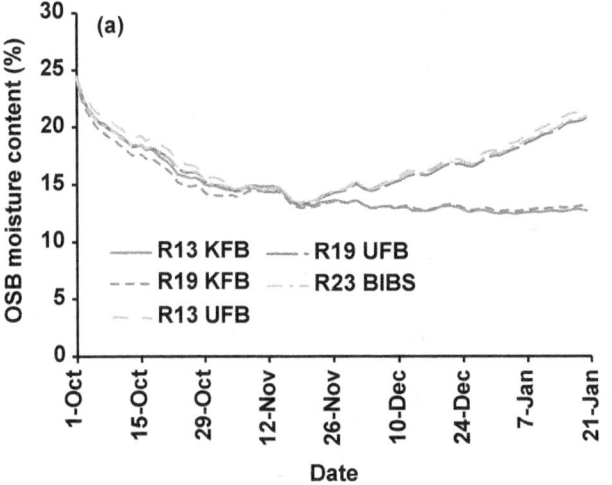

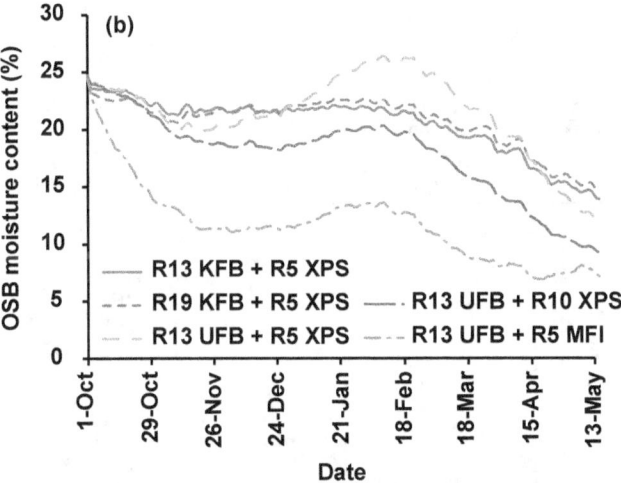

Figure 22. OSB drying performance in walls without (a) and with (b) exterior insulation.

and Straube (2011) for simulations of plywood sheathing in 2 by 6 wood-frame walls in the climate of Portland, Oregon (zone 4C).

4.2.2 Sensitivity of Drying Performance to Varying Parameters

This section investigates the effects of various parameters on the drying performance of OSB sheathing. Simulations were started on October 1 using the Baltimore warm year, an initial OSB moisture content of 25.6%, and the default parameters with variations given in Section 3.10.

Table 6 summarizes the influence of varying the different parameters on OSB drying performance. Drying performance is characterized here in terms of moisture content during the first two months, prior to wintertime moisture accumulation. Table 6 lists moisture content values at 7 weeks (November 19), which in most cases is the

minimum in moisture content after initial drying, prior to wintertime moisture accumulation.

The OSB drying rate in Wall 2 (R19 KFB) is insensitive to the vapor permeance of the asphalt-coated kraft facing. This implies that drying of the OSB is primarily in the outward direction. It also happens to be the case that for most of October and November outdoor vapor pressure is lower than indoor vapor pressure (Fig. 8).

The following observations are made regarding how the OSB drying rate in Wall 4 (R19 UFB) varies with selected parameters:

- Drying rate is insensitive to the vapor permeance of the latex primer/paint on the interior gypsum board.

- Drying rate is highly sensitive to the vapor permeance of the OSB itself. Higher permeance corresponds with faster drying rate, as moisture diffuses more rapidly out of the OSB.

- Drying rate is slightly sensitive to the vapor permeance of the spun bonded polyolefin membrane and to the equivalent vapor permeance of the vinyl siding. Higher permeance corresponds with faster drying rate.

- Drying rate is highly sensitive to wall orientation. The north-facing wall dries most slowly; the east- and west-facing walls are nearly identical; and the south-facing wall dries most rapidly.

- Drying rate is somewhat sensitive to indoor humidity levels. Higher (default) indoor humidity levels result in slower drying.

Drying of Wall 8 (R13 UFB + R5 XPS) is moderately sensitive to the vapor permeance of the exterior extruded polystyrene insulation. Higher permeance corresponds with faster drying rate, as moisture diffuses more rapidly out of the OSB through the XPS.

Ranking the sensitivity of the OSB drying rate using the metric of Table 6, it is most sensitive to wall orientation followed by OSB vapor permeance. Next in order of importance is indoor humidity level. Then vinyl siding equivalent vapor permeance, SBPO vapor permeance, and XPS vapor permeance have approximately the same influence. The drying performance metric is rather insensitive to primer/paint vapor permeance and kraft vapor permeance.

4.3 Effect of Wind-Driven Rain on OSB Moisture Content

Simulations are compared here for north-facing walls using the Baltimore warm year. Over the course of a year, 142 kg·m^{-2} of wind-driven rain strikes the north facing wall. The simulations look at cases where 0.5% and 1% of this incident wind-driven rain is deposited uniformly within the OSB layer. The results discussed below are particular to the weather file, wall orientation, and modeling assumptions.

Table 6. Summary of drying performance sensitivity analysis

Wall assembly	Parameter	Value	OSB moisture content (kg·kg⁻¹) after 7 weeks	Change from default (%)
R19 KFB		Default values	0.130	—
	Kraft vapor permeance	Low	0.129	− 0.6
		High	0.131	+ 0.6
R19 UFB		Default values	0.133	—
	Primer + paint vapor permeance	5 perms	0.135	+ 2
		20 perms	0.131	− 1
	OSB vapor permeance	×½	0.154	+ 16
		×2	0.120	− 9
	SBPO vapor permeance	25 perms	0.139	+ 5
		100 perms	0.130	− 2
	Vinyl siding equivalent vapor permeance	20 perms	0.140	+ 6
		80 perms	0.129	− 3
	Wall orientation	South	0.107	− 19
		East	0.123	− 7
		West	0.123	− 7
	Indoor humidity	Typical curve	0.119	− 10
R13 UFB	XPS vapor permeance	Default (0.76 perms)	0.199	—
+ R5 XPS		1.4 perms	0.188	−5

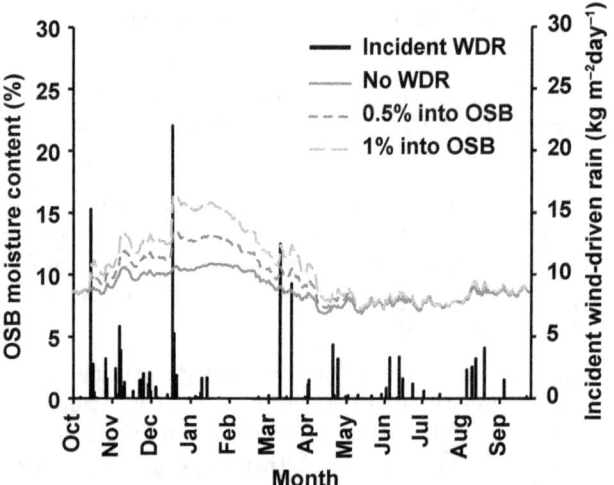

Figure 23. Effect of wind-driven rain intrusion on OSB moisture content in Wall 1 (R13 KFB). Daily values of incident wind-driven rain (right axis) were calculated by summing hourly values.

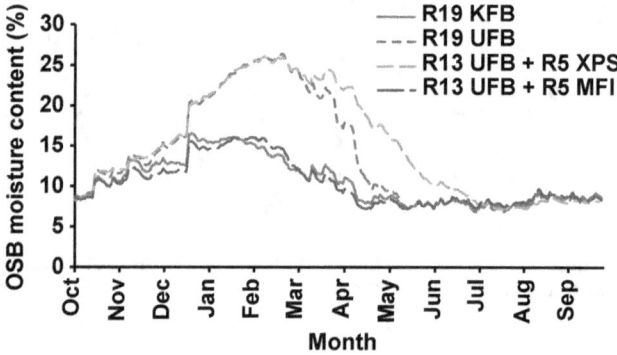

Figure 24. Effect of 1% wind-driven rain intrusion on OSB moisture content in various wall assemblies.

As stated previously, simulations were run for at least three years. Stable annual trends were found by the third year in all cases.

The moisture content of OSB in Wall 1 (R13 KFB) and the amount of incident wind-driven rain are shown in Figure 23. The major rain events occur in fall and winter. The steps in OSB moisture content with rain events are clearly evident.

For a rain event of a given intensity, OSB moisture content increases suddenly and then decreases more rapidly during warm weather than during cold weather because drying capability is greater at higher temperature (Section 4.2).

Figure 24 compares OSB moisture content in four selected wall assemblies with 1% wind-driven rain intrusion. Values for Walls 1 and 2 (R13 KFB, Figure 23, and R19 KFB, Figure 24) are practically identical. In Wall 4 (R19 UFB), wintertime vapor diffusion is dominant and has a greater effect on OSB moisture content than wind-driven rain. Walls 3 (R13 UFB) and 5 (R23 BIBS) behave similarly (not shown). Wall 8 (R13 UFB + R5 XPS) also behaves similarly except that it dries more slowly in the spring, as would be

Table 7. Effect of 1% wind-driven rain intrusion on OSB moisture content

Wall assembly	Maximum OSB moisture content (%)	Mean annual excess OSB moisture content (%)
1. R13 KFB	16.4	1.74
2. R19 KFB	16.6	1.78
3. R13 UFB	28.6	2.48
4. R19 UFB	26.4	2.05
5. R23 BIBS	26.6	2.07
6. R13 KFB + R5 XPS	20.3	5.69
7. R19 KFB + R5 XPS	21.7	6.23
8. R13 UFB + R5 XPS	26.1	4.18
9. R13 UFB + R10 XPS	20.5	3.23
10. R13 UFB + R5 MFI	16.1	1.25

expected from Section 4.2. Wall 10 (R13 UFB + R5 MFI) behaves similarly to Wall 2 (R19 KFB); both walls avoid excessive moisture accumulation from vapor diffusion and are able to accommodate this quantity of wind-driven rain because of their drying capability.

Table 7 summarizes the effect of 1% wind-driven rain intrusion on OSB moisture content in all 10 wall assemblies. It lists the maximum OSB moisture content in winter and the annual mean excess moisture content, which is the difference in OSB moisture content with 1% WDR intrusion relative to the case without WDR intrusion, averaged over one year. The trends in mean excess moisture content are similar to the drying performance trends discussed above in Section 4.2. Wall 10 (R13 UFB + R5 MFI) has the greatest capability to survive wind-driven rain intrusion, followed by Walls 1 and 2 (R13 KFB and R19 KFB). Walls 6 and 7 (R13 KFB + R5 XPS and R19 KFB + R5 XPS) have the highest mean MC excess (Table 7) and the slowest drying times (Table 5). Comparing Walls 8 and 9 (R13 UFB + R5 XPS and R13 UFB + R10 XPS), R10 XPS performs better than R5 XPS in that it lowers the wintertime maximum MC and lowers the mean annual excess MC, as expected from the trends in Sections 4.1 and 4.2.

Ueno (2010) conducted a similar hygrothermal analysis of the effect of a superinsulation retrofit on the capacity of a wall to dry after wind-driven rain penetration. In a Massachusetts climate (zone 5A), the original wall construction (nominal 2 by 4) could survive 0.5% penetration of incident wind-driven rain into the wood sheathing. The north-facing wall sheathing reached a maximum of 23% MC in winter and dried to below 10% MC in summer (repeatable annual cycle over three years). However, under the same rain penetration conditions, a retrofit wall with 100 mm (4 in.) of impermeable foil-faced rigid polyisocyanurate insulation exterior to the wood sheathing reduced its ability to dry; wood moisture content exceeded 30% by the third winter in the north-facing wall. A similar result was found when the same thickness of extruded polystyrene (XPS) was

substituted for polyisocyanurate. The same thickness of expanded polystyrene (EPS), however, resulted in lower winter moisture contents than the original wall under the same rain penetration conditions because EPS is more vapor permeable than XPS and polyisocyanurate. Although differences in climate and wall construction exist between this report and that of Ueno (2010), the trend with respect to vapor permeance of the exterior insulation is similar.

4.4 Effect of Air Exfiltration on OSB Moisture Content

Simulations are compared here for north-facing walls using the Baltimore warm year. These simulations look at air exfiltration with leakage coefficients of 0.02 and 0.04 $m^3 \cdot m^{-2} \cdot h^{-1} \cdot Pa^{-1}$, hereafter called "moderate exfiltration" and "excessive exfiltration," respectively. As discussed in Section 3.4, these airflows are still relatively small and do not violate the model assumption that air leakage does not significantly affect the sheathing temperature. As stated previously, simulations were run for at least 3 years. Stable annual trends were found by the third year in all cases.

Figure 25 compares the effect of air exfiltration on the moisture content of OSB for three different wall assemblies. Wall 1 (R13 KFB) undergoes a considerable increase in wintertime moisture accumulation when air exfiltration is included; Wall 6 (R13 KFB + R5 XPS) sees much less of an effect; and exfiltration has barely any effect on Wall 9 (R13 UFB + R10 XPS). The different effects of air exfiltration in these wall assemblies clearly result from the exterior insulation warming the OSB during winter, as discussed in Section 4.1.2.

Table 8 summarizes the effect of air exfiltration on OSB moisture content in all 10 wall assemblies. It gives the maximum OSB moisture content in winter as well as the amount of moisture deposited in OSB from air exfiltration. Equation 2 implies that the amount of moisture deposited in OSB depends on the rate of air leakage, the indoor humidity level, and the temperature of the OSB interior surface. The effect of the rate of air exfiltration is clear from Table 8. Other modeling studies (e.g., Ojanen and Kumaran 1992) have shown that moisture accumulation from air exfiltration is more severe when indoor humidity levels are higher.

Two temperature-related trends are highlighted here. First, walls with higher levels of cavity insulation accumulate slightly more moisture in the OSB sheathing than otherwise identical walls with lower levels of cavity insulation. This can be seen most clearly by contrasting Wall 6 (R13 KFB + R5 XPS) with Wall 7 (R19 KFB + R5 XPS). The trend also holds for Wall 1 (R13 KFB) vs. Wall 2 (R19 KFB) and for Wall 3 (R13 UFB) vs. Wall 4 (R19 UFB) vs. Wall 5 (R23 BIBS). Second, increasing the R-value of exterior insulation decreases the amount of moisture deposited by exfiltration. This trend can be seen by contrasting Wall 3 (no exterior insulation), Wall 8 (R5 XPS), and Wall 9 (R10 XPS).

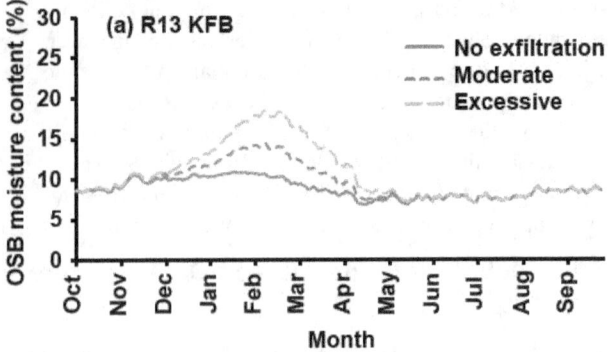

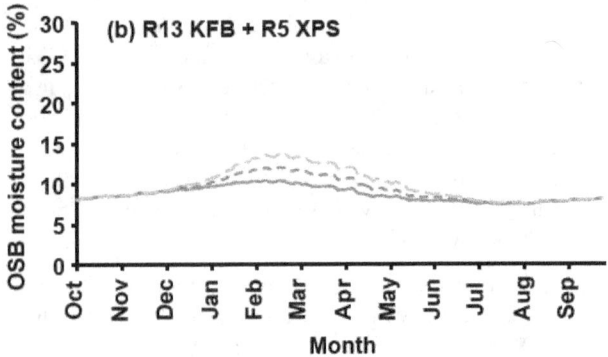

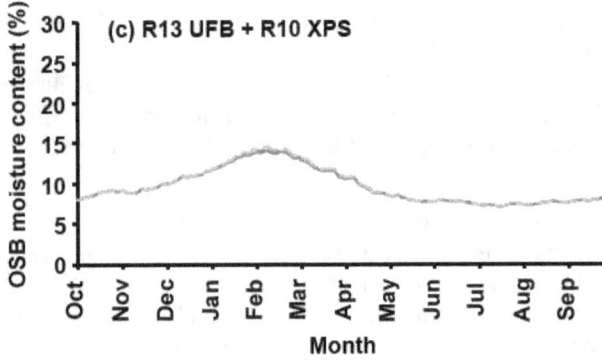

Figure 25. Effect of air exfiltration on OSB moisture content in (a) Wall 1, R13 KFB; (b) Wall 6, R13 KFB + R5 XPS; and (c) Wall 9, R13 UFB + R10 XPS.

5. Summary

5.1 Moisture Accumulation from Vapor Diffusion

All wall assemblies simulated in this study show a trend of higher OSB moisture content in winter and lower MC in summer. The critical parameters that affect wintertime MC are indoor humidity levels and vapor permeance of the interior of the wall assembly. Walls with kraft-faced batts have lower wintertime OSB moisture content (typically 10% to 11% MC) than walls with unfaced cavity insulation (typically 13% to 24% MC). Exterior insulation significantly lowers wintertime OSB moisture content in walls with unfaced cavity insulation.

In walls without exterior insulation, an interior vapor retarder appears to be necessary to avoid excessive wintertime moisture accumulation in OSB in north-facing walls under design indoor humidity conditions. Although a number of criteria are available for defining performance thresholds, this study does not attempt to address pass/fail criteria (see Section 1.3), and therefore does not set a threshold for permeance of the interior vapor retarder. Nonetheless it is noteworthy that OSB in Wall 2 (R19 KFB) simulated with "high" kraft permeance (3–4 perms) reaches a maximum of 14% MC, and that OSB in Wall 4 (R19 UFB) with primer and paint on interior gypsum board simulated at 5 perms reaches a maximum of 18% MC. When the latter wall is simulated with 10- and 20-perm interior finishes, wintertime MC rises to 23% and 28%, respectively.

Wall thickness and the R-value of cavity insulation have little effect on seasonal vapor diffusion trends in OSB moisture content.

Exterior insulation (XPS simulated at R5 and R10 and MFI at R5) dampens the seasonal trend in OSB moisture content. The maximum MC in winter and the minimum MC in summer occur later in time compared with otherwise identical walls without XPS or MFI. In addition, the wintertime MC is lower for walls with exterior insulation than

Table 8. Effect of different levels of air exfiltration on moisture accumulation in OSB

Wall assembly	Maximum OSB moisture content (%)			Amount of moisture deposited in OSB (kg m^{-2} yr^{-1})	
	No exfiltration	Moderate exfiltration	Excessive exfiltration	Moderate exfiltration	Excessive exfiltration
1. R13 KFB	10.9	14.4	18.4	0.44	0.87
2. R19 KFB	11.1	14.7	18.9	0.45	0.91
3. R13 UFB	23.6	27.7	32.5	0.43	0.86
4. R19 UFB	22.3	26.2	31.0	0.45	0.90
5. R23 BIBS	22.6	26.5	31.3	0.46	0.91
6. R13 KFB + R5 XPS	10.4	12.0	13.7	0.16	0.31
7. R19 KFB + R5 XPS	11.0	13.2	15.6	0.22	0.44
8. R13 UFB + R5 XPS	18.4	19.9	21.5	0.15	0.29
9. R13 UFB + R10 XPS	14.1	14.3	14.5	0.03	0.06
10. R13 UFB + R5 MFI	13.2	14.5	16.0	0.16	0.32

Table 9. Comparison of moisture performance

Wall assembly	Avoidance of moisture accumulation from vapor diffusion	Avoidance of moisture accumulation from air exfiltration	Drying capability	Ability to survive wind-driven rain penetration
1. R13 KFB	Excellent	Poor	Good	Good
2. R19 KFB	Excellent	Poor	Good	Good
3. R13 UFB	Poor	Poor	Good	Good
4. R19 UFB	Poor	Poor	Good	Good
5. R23 BIBS	Poor	Poor	Good	Good
6. R13 KFB + R5 XPS	Excellent	Good	Poor	Poor
7. R19 KFB + R5 XPS	Excellent	Fair	Poor	Poor
8. R13 UFB + R5 XPS	Fair	Good	Poor	Fair
9. R13 UFB + R10 XPS	Good	Excellent	Poor	Fair
10. R13 UFB + R5 MFI	Good	Good	Good	Excellent

otherwise identical walls without exterior insulation. OSB moisture content is considerably lower with R10 XPS than with R5 XPS; the greater the amount of exterior insulation, the warmer the OSB, and therefore the lower the relative humidity and moisture content. In addition, OSB moisture content is considerably lower with R5 mineral fiber insulation than with R5 extruded polystyrene. This difference occurs because MFI is vapor permeable, allowing water vapor to pass through the OSB to the exterior, whereas XPS is semi-impermeable.

Summertime inward vapor diffusion does not result in excessive cavity RH values, even when simulated with a low permeance kraft vapor retarder. However, all the walls were simulated with non-absorptive vinyl siding. Further analysis of inward vapor diffusion in walls with absorptive claddings in mixed-humid climates would be worthwhile.

5.2 OSB Drying Performance

The critical variables that affect OSB drying performance are the following:

- Time of year: drying occurs most rapidly in summer and most slowly in winter.

- Wall orientation: south-facing walls dry fastest, followed by east- and west-facing walls, with north-facing walls drying slowest.

- Vapor permeance of exterior wall components: walls with exterior XPS insulation dry much more slowly in all seasons than walls with exterior MFI insulation or walls without exterior insulation; the sensitivity analysis further indicates that the higher the vapor permeance of the OSB itself, the higher the drying rate; to a lesser extent, the higher the vapor permeance of the vinyl siding and the SBPO membrane, the higher the drying rate.

- Indoor humidity levels: drying is faster with lower indoor humidity levels.

OSB with a high initial moisture content dries primarily to the exterior for simulations starting on October 1. This is

evident from the sensitivity analysis, which shows that wall orientation and vapor permeance of OSB, SBPO membrane, and vinyl siding substantially affect drying rates. In addition, the sensitivity analysis shows that OSB drying rates depend minimally on the permeance of the kraft vapor retarder or the interior paint.

For simulations starting at other times of the year, outward drying of OSB also contributes significantly to the overall drying rate in walls with permeable exterior components. Walls with exterior XPS insulation dry at a much slower rate than walls with MFI or walls without exterior insulation. OSB in walls with XPS does dry to the interior in this climate (except during the four coldest months of the year), but the rate of inward drying is slow. Even in July, when inward drying would be expected to be most significant, walls with exterior XPS take about three to six times longer to dry than comparable walls without XPS. This is due partly to the low permeance of XPS and partly to a thermal effect. The thermal effect is evident in that the wall with permeable mineral fiber insulation takes about twice as long to dry in July than the comparable wall without MFI; at other times of year the drying rates for these walls are similar to each other. The exterior insulation cools the OSB and reduces heat flow to the OSB in July (when outdoors is warmer than indoors), thereby lowering the drying rate. The same trend exists for walls with different levels of XPS insulation: in summer drying is faster for R5 XPS than for R10 XPS. This trend reverses in fall and winter: drying is faster for R10 XPS than for R5 XPS because the OSB temperature is higher with R10 XPS.

5.3 Wind-Driven Rain Intrusion

The results discussed here are particular to several factors: the wall orientation was north-facing; the weather file had the major rain events during fall and winter; and the simulations assumed the intruding wind-driven rain went directly into the OSB layer. Under these assumptions, the ability of wall assemblies to dry in response to wind-driven rain penetration essentially reflects their drying capability from an initially high moisture content (see above). In response to a rain event of a given intensity, OSB moisture content remains elevated longer during cold weather than during warm weather because drying capability is greater at higher temperature. The annual mean excess moisture content was used as a metric, which is the difference in OSB moisture content with 1% WDR intrusion relative to the case without WDR intrusion, averaged over one year. In general, walls without exterior XPS insulation have a greater capability to dry after wind-driven rain intrusion than those with XPS. The best wall according to this metric was R13 UFB + R5 MFI; the worst wall was R19 KFB + R5 XPS. R13 UFB + R5 XPS performed better than R13 KFB + R5 XPS, and R13 UFB + R10 XPS performed better than R13 UFB + R5 XPS.

5.4 Air Exfiltration

The potential for wintertime moisture accumulation in OSB sheathing from air exfiltration relates to the rate of air leakage, the interior humidity levels, and the OSB interior surface temperature. Walls with higher levels of cavity insulation accumulate more moisture in the OSB than walls with lower levels of cavity insulation. Exterior insulation warms the OSB and decreases the amount of moisture deposited by air leakage.

5.5 Wall Assembly Performance Comparison

Table 9 summarizes hygrothermal performance in qualitative terms based on the metrics discussed above for vapor diffusion, air exfiltration, drying capability at various times of the year, and wind-driven rain intrusion. This provides a relative indication of the potential moisture performance risks associated with each assembly. However, it is not a quantitative risk assessment.

From this comparison, the following concluding remarks are made, as limited by the simulation assumptions discussed above:

- Walls with kraft vapor retarders and no exterior insulation perform well in all categories except risk of moisture accumulation from air exfiltration; however, these walls also have good drying capability, so the moisture accumulated from air leakage during cold weather dries rapidly in warmer weather.

- Walls with no kraft vapor retarder and no exterior insulation are prone to moisture accumulation from vapor diffusion and air leakage, though their drying capability is good.

- Low-perm extruded polystyrene exterior insulation impedes drying of OSB, and walls that include XPS have limited ability to dry out in the event of wind-driven rain penetration, particularly during cold weather. The exterior insulation helps avoid moisture accumulation from air exfiltration (and from vapor diffusion when a kraft

vapor retarder is lacking). The extent to which moisture accumulation is avoided improves as the ratio of exterior insulation to cavity insulation increases.

- Permeable rigid mineral fiber insulation does not impede the drying of OSB and has the same benefit as XPS in reducing moisture accumulation from air leakage and vapor diffusion. According to these metrics, the overall best performing wall assembly simulated in this study was Wall 10 (R13 UFB + R5 MFI). This assembly has good performance in all categories and has the highest capability to dry in response to wind-driven rain intrusion.

References

Antretter, F.; Holm, A.; Karagiozis, A.; Glass, S. 2010. Interior temperature and relative humidity distributions in mixed-humid and cold climates as building simulation boundary conditions. In: Proceedings: Thermal Performance of the Exterior Envelopes of Whole Buildings XI International Conference, Paper 133. Atlanta: American Society of Heating, Refrigerating and Air-Conditioning Engineers, Inc.

ASHRAE. 2009a. Criteria for moisture-control design analysis in buildings. ANSI/ASHRAE Standard 160-2009. Atlanta: American Society of Heating, Refrigerating and Air-Conditioning Engineers, Inc. 14 p.

ASHRAE. 2009b. Heat, air, and moisture control in building assemblies-Fundamentals. In: 2009 ASHRAE Handbook-Fundamentals. Atlanta: American Society of Heating, Refrigerating and Air-Conditioning Engineers, Inc. Chapter 25.

ASHRAE. 2009c. Heat, air, and moisture control in building assemblies-Material properties. In: 2009 ASHRAE Handbook-Fundamentals. Atlanta: American Society of Heating, Refrigerating and Air-Conditioning Engineers, Inc. Chapter 26.

BSC. 2010a. Building materials property table [Information Sheet Info-500]. Building Science Corporation. http://www.buildingscience.com/documents/information-sheets/building-materials-property-table. (15 January 2013).

BSC. 2010b. Vapor permeance of some building materials [Information Sheet Info-312]. Building Science Corporation. http://www.buildingscience.com/documents/information-sheets/info-312-vapor-permeance-some-materials. (15 January 2013).

Burch, D.M; TenWolde, A. 1993. A computer analysis of moisture accumulation in the walls of manufactured housing. ASHRAE Transactions. 99(2):977–990.

Burch, D.M.; Thomas, W.C.; Fanney, A.H. 1992. Water vapor permeability measurements of common building materials. ASHRAE Transactions. 98(2):486–494.

Carll, C.G.; Highley, T.L. 1999. Decay of wood and wood-based products above ground in buildings. Journal of Testing and Evaluation. 27(2):150–158.

Carll, C.; Wiedenhoeft, A.C. 2009. Moisture-related properties of wood and the effects of moisture on wood and wood products. In: Trechsel, H.R.; Bomberg, M.T., eds., Moisture control in buildings: the key factor in mold prevention, 2nd ed. West Conshohocken, PA: ASTM International: 54–79. Chapter 4.

Christian, J.E. 2009. Moisture sources. In: Trechsel, H.R.; Bomberg, M.T., eds., Moisture control in buildings: the key factor in mold prevention, 2nd ed. West Conshohocken, PA: ASTM International: 103–109. Chapter 7.

Dahl, S.D.; Kuehn, T.H.; Ramsey, J.W.; Yang, C.-H. 1996. Moisture storage and non-isothermal transport properties of common building materials. HVAC&R Research. 2(1):42–58.

Drumheller, S.C.; Carll, C. 2010. Effect of cladding systems on moisture performance of wood-framed walls in a mixed-humid climate. In: Proceedings: Thermal Performance of the Exterior Envelopes of Whole Buildings XI International Conference, Paper 49. Atlanta: American Society of Heating, Refrigerating and Air-Conditioning Engineers, Inc.

Dennis, J.K.; Zou, C.; Short, N.R. 1995. Corrosion behavior of zinc and zinc alloy coated steel in preservative treated timber. Transactions of the Institute of Metal Finishing. 73(3):96–101.

Derome, D. 2010. The nature, significance, and control of solar-driven diffusion in wall systems. Final report, Research Project RP-1235. Atlanta: American Society of Heating, Refrigerating and Air-Conditioning Engineers, Inc.

Gatland, S. 2005. Comparison of water vapor permeance data of common interior building materials in North American wall systems. In: Proceedings of the 10th Canadian Conference on Building Science and Technology, Ottawa, ON, pp. 182–194.

Gibson, S. 2010. Can exterior foam insulation cause mold and moisture problems? Green Building Advisor. http://www.greenbuildingadvisor.com/blogs/dept/qa-spotlight/can-exterior-foam-insulation-cause-mold-and-moisture-problems. (15 January 2013).

Glass, S.V.; TenWolde, A. 2007. Review of in-service moisture and temperature conditions in wood-frame buildings. General Technical Report FPL-GTR-174. Madison, WI: U.S. Department of Agriculture, Forest Service, Forest Products Laboratory. 53 p.

Glass, S.V.; TenWolde, A. 2009. Review of moisture balance models for residential indoor humidity. In: Proceedings of the 12th Canadian Conference on Building Science and Technology, Vol. 1:231–245. Montréal: Québec Building Envelope Council.

Glass, S.V.; Zelinka, S.L. 2010. Moisture relations and physical properties of wood. In: Ross, R.J., ed., Wood handbook-Wood as an engineering material. General Technical Report FPL–GTR–190. Madison, WI: U.S. Department of Agriculture, Forest Service, Forest Products Laboratory. Chapter 4.

Hagentoft, C.-E.; Harderup, E. 1996. Moisture conditions in a north facing wall with cellulose loose fill insulation: Constructions with and without vapor retarder and air leakage. Journal of Thermal Insulation and Building Envelopes. 19:228–243.

Hartley, I.D.; Wang, S.; Zhang, Y. 2007. Water vapor sorption isotherm modeling of commercial oriented strand panel based on species groups and resin type. Building and Environment. 42:3655–3659.

Hens, H. 1990. Guidelines and practice. International Energy Agency Annex XIV: Condensation and Energy, Vol. 2. Leuven, Belgium: K.U. Leuven, Laboratory for Building Physics.

Hens, H. 1996. Final Report, Vol. 1, Task 1: Modelling. International Energy Agency Annex 24-Heat, Air and Moisture Transfer Through New and Retrofitted Insulated Envelope Parts (HAMTIE). Leuven, Belgium: Katholieke Universiteit Leuven, Departement Burgerlijke Bouwkunde, Laboratorium Bouwfysica.

IBP. 2011. WUFI® Pro version 5.1. Holzkirchen, Germany: Fraunhofer Institute for Building Physics. http://www.wufi.de/index_e html. (15 January 2013).

Kalamees, T.; Kurnitski, J. 2010. Moisture convection performance of external walls and roofs. Journal of Building Physics. 33(3):225–247.

Karagiozis, A.N. 2001. Advanced numerical models for hygrothermal research. In: Trechsel, H.R., ed., Moisture analysis and condensation control in building envelopes. ASTM MNL40. West Conshohocken, PA: American Society for Testing and Materials: 90–106. Chapter 6.

Karagiozis, A.; Wilkes, K. 2004. Hygrothermal properties of selected materials. Report 2, ASHRAE Research Project 1091, Development of design strategies for rainscreen and sheathing membrane performance in wood frame walls. Atlanta: American Society of Heating, Refrigerating and Air-Conditioning Engineers, Inc.

Kumaran, M.K. 1996. Material properties. Final Report, Vol. 3, Task 3. International Energy Agency Annex 24-Heat, Air and Moisture Transfer Through New and Retrofitted Insulated Envelope Parts (HAMTIE). Leuven, Belgium: Katholieke Universiteit Leuven, Departement Burgerlijke Bouwkunde, Laboratorium Bouwfysica.

Kumaran, M.K. 2001. Hygrothermal properties of building materials. In: Trechsel, H.R., ed., Moisture analysis and condensation control in building envelopes. ASTM MNL40. West Conshohocken, PA: American Society for Testing and Materials: 29–65. Chapter 3.

Kumaran, M.K. 2009. Fundamentals of transport and storage of moisture in building materials and components. In: Trechsel, H.R.; Bomberg, M.T., eds., Moisture control in buildings: the key factor in mold prevention, 2nd ed. West Conshohocken, PA: ASTM International: 1–15. Chapter 1.

Kumaran, M.K., J.C. Lackey, N. Normandin, F. Tariku, and D. van Reenen. 2002. A thermal and moisture transport property database for common building and insulation materials. Final Report, ASHRAE Research Project RP-1018. Atlanta: American Society of Heating, Refrigerating and Air-Conditioning Engineers, Inc.

Künzel, H.M. 1995. Simultaneous heat and moisture transport in building components: one- and two-dimensional calculation using simple parameters. Stuttgart, Germany: Fraunhofer IRB Verlag.

Martin, P.C.; Verschoor, J.D. 1994. Investigation of water vapor migration and moisture storage in an insulated wall structure. Final Report, ASHRAE Research Project 496-RP. Atlanta: American Society of Heating, Refrigerating and Air-Conditioning Engineers, Inc.

MHRA. 2000. Measured permeance values for selected interior wall assemblies. New York: Manufactured Housing Research Alliance. http://www.research-alliance.org/pages/perm htm. (15 January 2013).

Ojanen, T.; Ahonen, J.; Simonson, C.J. 2006. Moisture performance characteristics of OSB and spruce plywood exterior sheathing products. In: Fazio, P.; Ge, H.; Rao, J.; Desmarais, G., eds., Research in building physics and building engineering: Proceedings of the third international building physics conference. London: Taylor & Francis: 97–105.

Ojanen, T.; Kumaran, M.K. 1992. Air exfiltration and moisture accumulation in residential wall cavities. In: Proceedings: Thermal Performance of the Exterior Envelopes of Buildings V International Conference. Atlanta: American Society of Heating, Refrigerating and Air-Conditioning Engineers, Inc.: 491–500.

Ojanen, T.; Kumaran, K. 1996. Effect of exfiltration on the hygrothermal behaviour of a residential wall assembly. Journal of Thermal Insulation and Building Envelopes. 19:215–227.

NAHB Research Center. 2010. Moisture performance of wood-based sheathing on exterior walls clad with absorptive materials. Report prepared for U.S. Forest Products Laboratory and U.S. Department of Housing and Urban Development. http://www.toolbase.org/PDF/CaseStudies/Moisture-PerformanceWoodBasedSheathing.pdf . (15 January 2013).

Richards, R.F.; Burch, D.M.; Thomas, W.C. 1992. Water vapor sorption measurements of common building materials. ASHRAE Transactions. 98(2):117–127.

Smegal, J.; Straube, J. 2011. Hygrothermal analysis of exterior rockwool insulation. Research Report 1104. Somerville, MA: Building Science Press.

Straube, J. 2011. Controlling cold-weather condensation using insulation. Building Science Digest 163. Somerville, MA: Building Science Press. 8 p.

Straube, J.; Burnett, E. 2001. Overview of hygrothermal (HAM) analysis methods. In: Trechsel, H.R., ed., Moisture analysis and condensation control in building envelopes. West Conshohocken, PA: American Society for Testing and Materials: 81–89. Chapter 5.

Straube, J.F.; Burnett, E.F.P. 2005. Building science for building enclosures. Westford, MA: Building Science Press. 542 p.

Tariku, F.; Cornick, S.M.; Lacasse, M.A. 2007. Simulation of wind-driven rain penetration effects on the performance of a stucco-clad wall. In: Proceedings: Thermal Performance of the Exterior Envelopes of Whole Buildings X International Conference, Paper 198. Atlanta: American Society of Heating, Refrigerating and Air-Conditioning Engineers, Inc.

TenWolde, A. 2011. A review of ASHRAE Standard 160-Criteria for moisture control design analysis in buildings. Journal of Testing and Evaluation. 39(1). doi:10.1520/JTE102896.

TenWolde, A.; Bomberg, M.T. 2009. Design tools. In: Trechsel, H.R.; Bomberg, M.T., eds., Moisture control in buildings: the key factor in mold prevention, 2nd ed. West Conshohocken, PA: ASTM International: 128–138. Chapter 10.

TenWolde, A.; Walker, I.S. 2001. Interior moisture design loads for residences. In: Proceedings: Performance of Exterior Envelopes of Whole Buildings VIII International Conference, Paper 33. Atlanta: American Society of Heating, Refrigerating and Air-Conditioning Engineers, Inc.

Thompson, A.; Taylor, B.N. 2008. Guide for the use of the International System of Units (SI). NIST Special Publication 811. Gaithersburg, MD: National Institute of Standards and Technology.

Timusk, P.C.; Pressnail, K.D.; Cooper, P.A. 2009. The effects of board density, resin content and component layers on the permeability properties of mill-fabricated oriented strandboard. In: Proceedings of the 12th Canadian Conference on Building Science and Technology, Vol. 1:325–334. Montréal: Québec Building Envelope Council.

Trechsel, H.R., ed. 2001. Moisture analysis and condensation control in building envelopes. ASTM MNL40. West Conshohocken, PA: American Society for Testing and Materials.

Tsongas, G.A.; Nelson, G.D. 1991. A field test for correlation of air leakage and high moisture content sites in tightly built walls. ASHRAE Transactions. 97(1):1–8.

Ueno, K. 2010. Residential exterior wall superinsulation retrofit details and analysis. In: Proceedings: Thermal Performance of the Exterior Envelopes of Whole Buildings XI International Conference, Paper 200. Atlanta: American Society of Heating, Refrigerating and Air-Conditioning Engineers, Inc.

Viitanen, H.; Salonvaara, M. 2001. Failure criteria. In: Trechsel, H.R., ed., Moisture analysis and condensation control in building envelopes. ASTM MNL40. West Conshohocken, PA: American Society for Testing and Materials: 66–80. Chapter 4.

Wiehagen, J. 2011. Personal communication. Energy Engineer, NAHB Research Center, 400 Prince Georges Blvd., Upper Marlboro, MD 20774.

Woloszyn, M.; Rode, C. 2008. IEA Annex 41: Whole building heat, air, moisture response, Subtask 1: Modelling principles and common exercises. International Energy Agency, Executive Committee on Energy Conservation in Buildings and Community Systems.